"A work of muscular grace and power ing tidal score by Tom Kitt and Brian Yc electric momentum of a rock opera—. on Broadway makes as direct a grab for the heart—or wrings it as thoroughly. Simply to describe what occurs doesn't do justice to the excitement this show generates. It is a brave and breathtaking musical."

—Ben Brantley, *New York Times*

"Incongruously, sometimes agonizingly, beautiful. Grade: A!"

—Melissa Rose Bernardo, *Entertainment Weekly*

"Next to wondrous! Tom Kitt and Brian Yorkey have created an exceptional show that says something meaningful and powerful. These songwriters' words and melodies resonate after you leave the theater."

—Joe Dziemianowicz, *Daily News*

"A startling, emotion-drenched musical about one family's attempt to cope with mental illness. The show is an impressive achievement, a heartfelt entertainment that tackles the uncomfortable subject of manic depression with a straightforwardness that is commendable. And it's emotional, too, in that Brian Yorkey, who wrote the book and lyrics, and Tom Kitt, who composed the music, have crafted an affecting contemporary tale that doesn't shortchange character or plot in their attempt to tell a difficult story."

—Michael Kuchwara, Associated Press

"*next to normal* offers a welcome, indie-like reminder that Broadway musicals can be about people rather than pyrotechnics."

—Brendan Lemon, *Financial Times*

"Its choice of subject alone is reason to admire *next to normal*. Too many small-scale musicals think even smaller. But the creative team here poses a potentially hackneyed question—Is it better to feel pain or smother it?—and gives it freshness, urgency and emotional integrity."

—David Rooney, *Variety*

"*next to normal* is that truly rare beast in the Broadway song and dance jungle: a creation with heart, guts and brains, served up in equal proportion. Not since *Spring Awakening* has a musical come along that quickens the pulse rate like this one does. With amazing balance, the book by Brian Yorkey (who also penned the often witty, always sensible lyrics) avoids the pitfalls of melodrama and sentimentality, letting us see these people in the raw, ragged state where years of living on the edge have left them."

—Richard Ouzounian, *Toronto Star*

"Rock is alive and rolling like thunder in *next to normal*. It is mesmerizing—an emotional powerhouse with a fire in its soul and a wicked wit that burns just as fiercely. Composer Tom Kitt and writer-lyricist Brian Yorkey have broken the shackles of tired Broadway tradition, pushing it in new directions. Next time you think the Broadway musical is dead, head off to *next to normal*. It'll pin you to your seat."
—**Peter Travers, *Rolling Stone***

"A perfect musical. Simply put, *next to normal* is truly one of the most powerful, surprising and invigorating original musicals in recent memory." —**Matt Windman, *am New York***

"A gutsy, unconventional Broadway show. This is not only a serious, substantial, dignified and musically sophisticated new American work, but a frequently moving picture of an empathetic nuclear family whose members are struggling, like many of us, to take care of themselves and each other, and to keep the stitches in the fraught fabric of their daily lives." —**Chris Jones, *Chicago Tribune***

"I was surprised—jaw-droppingly so—by *next to normal*, a musical about the effects of manic depression that is, appropriately enough, leaving audiences both teary-eyed and elated at Arena Stage's Crystal City theater. *next to normal* is about smart people who deal with tricky issues of love and loss and who do so in soaring, searing melodies, in ways that prove exhilarating and roundly affecting." —**Bob Mondello, *Washington City Paper***

"*next to normal* is that rare musical that touches your heart and gets under your skin. It's a great collaborative effort. Tom Kitt, who composed the music, with Brian Yorkey, crafting the lyrics and book, propel the story to fanciful and emotional heights." —**Roma Torre, NY1**

"A fresh, intelligent, compassionate and extremely touching experience. Tom Kitt's music and lyrics by Brian Yorkey probe the characters' minds and motivation with great psychological understanding. An exciting leap into the possibilities of musical theater." —**Robert Feldberg, *Record* (New Jersey)**

"A seamless, riveting, must-see event. *next to normal* artfully zooms in on a family in crisis, and the things that cripple them—denial, numbness, the refusal to examine difficult issues—things that often cripple modern musical theater audiences. Kitt and Yorkey's irresistible story will grab you and force you to look, listen and feel." —**Amy Krivohlavek, *Show Business Weekly***

next to normal

next to normal

music

Tom Kitt

book and lyrics

Brian Yorkey

theatre communications group
new york
2010

next to normal is published by Theatre Communications Group, Inc.,
520 Eighth Avenue, 24th Floor, New York, NY 10018–4156

This publication is made possible in part with public funds from the New York State Council on the Arts, a State Agency.

TCG books are exclusively distributed to the book trade by Consortium Book Sales and Distribution.

Library of Congress Cataloging-in-Publication Data
Kitt, Tom.
[Next to normal. Libretto]
Next to normal / music, Tom Kitt ; book and lyrics, Brian Yorkey.
p. cm.
ISBN 978-1-55936-370-9
1. Musicals—Librettos. I. Yorkey, Brian. II. Title.
ML50.K624N4   2010
782.1'40268—dc22   2010021764

Cover design by Lisa Govan
Cover image by Serino Coyne
Text design and composition by Lisa Govan

First Edition, June 2010

contents

Acknowledgments

ix

Foreword
By Anthony Rapp

xi

next to normal

1

acknowledgments

next to normal has been an unlikely project from the very start, and as its authors, we owe debts of gratitude to far too many people to list in a book this size.

But you wouldn't be holding this book in your hands at all if it weren't for producer extraordinaire David Stone, who believed in the show, and in us, long past the point others would have given up.

The same goes for the smart and passionate Michael Greif, who cared deeply about every word, every note, every moment, and brought our show to brilliant life.

The amazing producers, actors, designers and stage managers listed on the following pages have each made indelible contributions to the strange and wonderful journey of this show, and we thank them. Many others contributed to readings and workshops along the way, and we are grateful to each and every one of them as well.

The Jonathan Larson Performing Arts Foundation provided support at an essential time; thanks to Nancy Kassak Diekmann and the Larson family.

Thanks to Kurt Deutsch, Noah Cornman, Steve Norman and everyone at Sh-K-Boom records, early and ongoing supporters.

Peter Askin and James Lapine guided us in finding what the show wanted to be, and believed we could get it there, which meant the world to us.

acknowledgments

So did Carole Rothman, Chris Burney and everyone at Second Stage, and Molly Smith, David Dower and everyone at Arena Stage. Dr. Anthony Pietropinto, Dr. Nancy Elman and Dr. Quentin Van Meter provided invaluable medical advice, though any errors are ours alone.

Laura Pietropinto, Tom D'Ambrosio and Brandon Ivie looked out for us at moments of great overwhelmedness.

Anthony Rapp and Alex Lacamoire are awesome human beings.

next to normal was presented in an early form at the New York Musical Theatre Festival (Isaac Hurwitz, Executive Director) under the title *feeling electric*, produced by Reno Productions and Terry Byrne, Kristin Kopp and Amanda DuBois.

feeling electric was developed at Village Theatre in Issaquah, Washington (Robb Hunt, Executive Producer; Steve Tomkins, Artistic Director), and was subsequently presented in concert form at the Cutting Room in New York City (produced by Kurt Deutsch, Melissa Justin and Sh-K-Boom Records) and by Musical Mondays (Bick Goss, Artistic Director, and Frank Evans, Producing Director).

The show was born in the BMI-Lehman Engel Musical Theatre Workshop, and our gratitude and great respect go to Jean Banks, Maury Yeston, Skip Kennon and everyone there, with special remembrance of Richard Engquist, a mentor and a gentleman.

Thanks to Howard and Judy Kitt for their support throughout the years, and to the Kitt, Pietropinto and Yorkey families for standing by us and never telling us to get a real job.

Last and most, eternal thanks to John Buzzetti, the king of Broadway, and Joy Gorman, his queen.

foreword

There's something about the quintessentially American art form known as musical theater that can either drive me crazy or melt my heart forever. Even though my biggest successes as an actor have come in musicals, I've always sympathized with some folks' allergic reactions to the cornball razzamatazz of the old-school shows like *42nd Street* (although I do enjoy a good tap number) or *The Music Man* (although as a kid I did my best to memorize and emulate Robert Preston's indelible delivery of "Ya Got Trouble"). Instead, I've always been much more drawn to what I consider the breakthrough shows: *Gypsy*, *West Side Story* and *Sweeney Todd*, shows that honor many of the traditions of musical theater—a remarkable combination of music, lyric, dialogue and dance—but turn some of those traditions on their heads to venture into the darker, more complex corners of the human heart.

In 1994, after quite a few years in the business—most of which had been spent not doing any musical theater—I was fortunate to get the role of Mark Cohen in the latest breakthrough musical, a rock opera called *Rent*. Written by a young man in his thirties, Jonathan Larson, it was that rare thing in musical theater: a show that spoke directly to me about the world I lived in. It utilized music that sounded more like the modern rock I listened to than anything from traditional musical theater, and featured characters that reflected the lives of myself and my friends.

I hadn't known anyone was even attempting to write a musical like it, let alone succeeding. But what was especially exciting about *Rent* wasn't simply that it was modern; it also had an undeniable emotional power, a compelling story, and an irresistible life force running through it. And did I mention the music? I relished the opportunity to help bring it to fruition.

Rent's journey—beginning in obscurity at New York Theatre Workshop, moving to Broadway in a flurry of publicity, winning multiple Tony awards and a Pulitzer Prize, and becoming one of the longest running shows in Broadway history—has been well documented. The untimely and tragic death of Jonathan Larson, right before *Rent* premiered Off-Broadway in 1996, has also been well documented. But when we began rehearsals under the generous, collaborative and inventive vision of our director Michael Greif, we couldn't know what was to come. We just put our purest hearts and minds and talents together and did our very best work, and hoped that it would connect with the folks who came to bear witness to it.

Well, it certainly did connect with many, many, many folks, all over the world. Over the last fourteen years, *Rent* has changed a lot of people's lives, my own included, in every way possible. I've long said that if *Rent* were the last great project I were a part of, I could die satisfied. Of course, I hoped that I would come across something else that was special, but I knew that it was unlikely—*Rent* was a once in a lifetime show.

And then, in 2005, I was asked to do a workshop of another new rock musical. Called *feeling electric* (which became *next to normal*), it was to be a part of the nascent New York Musical Theatre Festival. I had worked on a reading of another show with its authors, two very cool young men named Tom Kitt and Brian Yorkey, so without hearing anything of its score, and after doing a quick perusal of its very promising script, I said yes.

It turned out that I had just become part of yet another once in a lifetime show, one, like *Rent*, that dared to tell a story that on paper might seem unlikely material for a musical. Manic depression? Delusional behavior? Electric shock therapy? It featured all of those things and more, but it worked beyond reason, because Tom and Brian never shied away from finding a way to express the core truths of what living with all of those difficult circumstances meant. And once again, as with *Rent*, I was blessed to sing songs that expressed these matters of life and death in a musical vocabulary that captured the feel and sounds of my favorite artists. How could I be so lucky as to have stumbled into yet another beautiful, moving, thrilling, once in a lifetime, break-through show?

During our rehearsal process, Tom and Brian shared with me that they had been deeply inspired by what Jonathan Larson had done for the medium of musical theater, and I know that Jonathan would in turn be as inspired by what they had done. I so wish he could see it.

The journeys of *Rent* and *next to normal* are similar in many ways: both began as deeply personal projects that were born out of their authors' desire to tell a meaningful, emotionally complex story, and both began their lives in a messy but thrilling state, undeniable in their power but very much in need of a sure hand to help them iron out their various creases. Both found that sure hand in Michael Greif. I've long felt that Michael has been the unsung hero in the story of *Rent*'s success, so I'm very happy that he's starting to get his due with regard to *next to normal*. I didn't continue on in a performing capacity as *feeling electric* became *next to normal* in the winter of 2008, but I did have the honor of serving as Michael's assistant during its Second Stage run, and saw firsthand his remarkable capacity not only to see what was missing in the piece, but to communicate it to Brian and Tom in a way that they could then be inspired to do even more brilliant work to make it better.

Credit must be given to its producer David Stone. He was steadfast in his belief that the show could work, and gave it the time and space it needed to fulfill its potential. He took wonderful care of his incredible cast—Alice, Brian, Jennifer, Aaron, Adam and Asa—as they made their way on the somewhat winding road from Second Stage to the Arena Stage in D.C. to Broadway. It was in no way a foregone conclusion that *next to normal* would find commercial success on Broadway, but David, Patrick Catullo and their other producing partners took a risk born of belief in its power, and have been rewarded for it. All of this patience and care on the part of producers is rare in show business these days; in a way, it's sort of the manner in which old-school producers used to work. Old-school methods for a break-through show.

This past April, when *next to normal* became the out-of-nowhere surprise pick as winner of the 2010 Pulitzer Prize for Drama, I couldn't help but feel that the ties that bound it to *Rent* had come full circle. I never got to congratulate Jonathan on his award back in 1996, since he had passed away a couple of months before it was announced, so it was with a very glad heart that I was able this time to join a dinner party in honor of my two friends Brian and Tom—young men who fervently believed in the power of musical theater to tell a meaningful story that could change people's lives—and raise a toast in celebration.

When writing musicals—at least as far as I can tell, given the material that is presented to me—it's easy to be clever, it's easy to be corny, it's easy to take the easy way out. It takes guts to get to the heart of the matter, to not flinch away from the painful truths and heartbreaks that we all live through. It takes guts to write about love and life and death and grief and joy. Thankfully, Jonathan Larson had those guts, and Tom and Brian have those guts. I cannot wait to see what new once in a lifetime story they decide to tell next. Hopefully I'll get to be a part of it. I should be so lucky.

Anthony Rapp
New York City
June 2010

next to normal

production history

The world premiere of *next to normal* was produced in January 2008 by Second Stage Theatre (Carole Rothman, Artistic Director; Ellen Richard, Executive Director). It was directed by Michael Greif with musical staging by Sergio Trujillo. The set design was by Mark Wendland, the costume design was by Jeff Mahshie, the lighting design was by Kevin Adams, the sound design was by Brian Ronan; the music director was Mary-Mitchell Campbell; the orchestrations were by Michael Starobin and Tom Kitt, the vocal arrangements were by AnnMarie Milazzo; the music coordinator was Michael Keller, the production stage manager was Judith Schoenfeld and the stage manager was Lori Ann Zepp. The cast was:

DIANA	Alice Ripley
GABE	Aaron Tveit
DAN	Brian d'Arcy James
NATALIE	Jennifer Damiano
HENRY	Adam Chanler-Berat
DOCTOR MADDEN/DOCTOR FINE	Asa Somers

next to normal was produced in November 2008 by Arena Stage (Molly Smith, Artistic Director; Edgar Dobie, Managing Director). It was directed by Michael Greif with musical staging by Sergio Trujillo. The set design was by Mark Wendland, the costume design was by Jeff Mahshie, the lighting design was by Kevin Adams, the sound design was by Brian Ronan; the music director was Charlie Alterman; the orchestrations were by Michael

Starobin and Tom Kitt, drums and additional percussion arrangements were by Damien Bassman, the vocal arrangements were by AnnMarie Milazzo; the production stage manager was Judith Schoenfeld and the assistant stage managers were Kurt Hall and Kathryn L. McKee. The cast was

DIANA	Alice Ripley
GABE	Aaron Tveit
DAN	J. Robert Spencer
NATALIE	Jennifer Damiano
HENRY	Adam Chanler-Berat
DOCTOR MADDEN/DOCTOR FINE	Louis Hobson

next to normal opened on Broadway in April 2009 at the Booth Theatre where it was presented by David Stone, James L. Nederlander, Barbara Whitman, Patrick Catullo and Second Stage Theatre. It was directed by Michael Greif with musical staging by Sergio Trujillo. The set design was by Mark Wendland, the costume design was by Jeff Mahshie, the lighting design was by Kevin Adams, the sound design was by Brian Ronan; the music director was Charlie Alterman; the orchestrations were by Michael Starobin and Tom Kitt, the vocal arrangements were by AnnMarie Milazzo; the music coordinator was Michael Keller, the production stage manager was Judith Schoenfeld and the stage manager was Martha Donaldson. The cast was:

DIANA	Alice Ripley
GABE	Aaron Tveit
DAN	J. Robert Spencer
NATALIE	Jennifer Damiano
HENRY	Adam Chanler-Berat
DOCTOR MADDEN/DOCTOR FINE	Louis Hobson

characters

DIANA   Sexy. Sharp. Delusional bipolar depressive.
                   Thirties or forties.

GABE   Her son. Dashing. Gentle. Bright. Playful.
                   Everything a mother, etc. Almost eighteen.

DAN   Her husband. Handsome. Genuine. Constant.
                   Tired. Thirties or forties.

NATALIE   Her daughter. Sixteen and trying to be per-
                   fect. It's not going well.

HENRY   Musician. Romantic. Stoner. Slacker. Philo-
                   sopher king. Seventeen.

DOCTOR MADDEN   On the young side of ageless. Assured. A rock
                   star.

Voices, Anesthesiologist, Nurses, Doctors and others are all
played by the company. A Psychopharmacologist (Doctor Fine)
is played by the actor playing Doctor Madden.

songs

Act One

Prelude (Light)	*Band*
Just Another Day	*Diana, Natalie, Gabe, Dan*
Everything Else	*Natalie*
Who's Crazy / My Psychopharmacologist and I	*Dan, Diana, Doctor Fine, Voices*
Perfect for You	*Henry, Natalie*
I Miss the Mountains	*Diana*
It's Gonna Be Good	*Dan, Gabe, Henry, Natalie*
He's Not Here	*Dan*
You Don't Know	*Diana*
I Am the One	*Dan, Gabe*
Superboy and the Invisible Girl	*Natalie, Diana, Gabe*
I'm Alive	*Gabe*
Make Up Your Mind / Catch Me I'm Falling	*Doctor Madden, Dan, Gabe, Diana, Natalie*
I Dreamed a Dance	*Diana, Gabe*
There's a World	*Gabe*
I've Been	*Dan, Gabe*
Didn't I See This Movie?	*Diana*
A Light in the Dark	*Dan, Diana*

Act Two

Wish I Were Here	*Diana, Natalie*
Song of Forgetting	*Dan, Diana, Natalie*
Hey #1	*Henry, Natalie*
Seconds and Years	*Doctor Madden, Dan, Diana*
Better Than Before	*Doctor Madden, Dan, Diana, Natalie*
Aftershocks	*Gabe, Diana*
Hey #2	*Henry, Natalie*
You Don't Know (Reprise)	*Diana, Doctor Madden*
How Could I Ever Forget?	*Diana, Dan*
It's Gonna Be Good (Reprise)	*Dan, Diana*
Why Stay?	*Diana, Natalie*
A Promise	*Dan, Henry*
I'm Alive (Reprise)	*Gabe*
The Break	*Diana*
Make Up Your Mind / Catch Me I'm Falling (Reprise)	*Doctor Madden, Diana, Gabe*
Maybe (Next to Normal)	*Diana, Natalie*
Hey #3 / Perfect for You (Reprise)	*Henry, Natalie*
So Anyway	*Diana*
I Am the One (Reprise)	*Dan, Gabe*
Light	*Full Company*

act one

prelude (light)

Music.
Then the lights go out.
A moment, and Diana turns on a light. She sits alone in a chair,
waiting.
Gabe enters.

GABE: What are you doing up? It's three-thirty.

just another day

DIANA:
It's the seventh night this week I've sat till morning . . .

GABE: Great. Here we go.

DIANA:
Imagining the ways you might have died.

GABE: Ah, yes, and tonight's winner is?

7

DIANA:

In a freak September ice storm with no warning . . .

GABE: Because that happens.

DIANA:

There's a gang war, there's a bird flu, trains collide.

GABE: What'd we say about watching the news?

DIANA:

Now you act all sweet and surly,
But you swore you'd come home early
And you lied.

GABE: You gotta let go, Mom—I'm almost eighteen.
DIANA: Are you snorting coke?
GABE: Not at the moment.
DAN *(Off)*: Who's up at this hour?
DIANA: Your father. Go. Up the back way.
GABE *(Going)*: Why does he hate me?
DIANA: Because you're a little twat.
GABE: You can't call me a twat.

(But she shoos him off as Dan enters.)

DAN: Everything okay? I heard voices.
DIANA: Just me. Talking to myself, you know. Now you head on
    upstairs—I'll be up for sex in a minute.
DAN: You'll . . . uh . . . are you sure you're okay?
DIANA: Go.

(She ushers him off, then sings:)

They're the perfect loving fam'ly, so adoring . . .
And I love them ev'ry day of ev'ry week.
So my son's a little shit, my husband's boring,
And my daughter, though a genius, is a freak.

> Still I help them love each other
> Father, mother, sister, brother,
> Cheek to cheek!

(Natalie enters, the way Gabe just left, with a pile of books and a tallboy of Red Bull, muttering to herself.)

Natalie? It's four in the morning—is everything okay?
NATALIE: Everything's great. Why wouldn't it be great? It's great. I've just got three more chapters of calculus, a physics problem set, a history quiz and two pages on floral imagery in *Flowers for Algernon* which is like duh. Everything's so under control it's just like . . . calm.

(She gulps from the can.)

DIANA: Honey, you need to slow down, take some time for yourself. I'm going to have sex with your father.
NATALIE: Great. Thanks. I'm so glad I know that.

(Diana goes; Natalie drops the books on a table and sings:)

> So it's times like these I wonder how I take it,
> And if other fam'lies live the way we do—
> If they love each other, or if they just fake it,
> And if other daughters feel like I feel, too.
>
> 'Cause some days I think I'm dying
> But I'm really only trying to get through.

(Gabe is in his room, before a mirror, getting dressed for the day.)

GABE:

> For just another day . . .
> For another stolen hour
> When the world will feel my power and obey.

GABE AND NATALIE:

> It's just another day . . .

GABE:

Feeling like I'll live forever . . .

NATALIE:

Feeling like this feeling never goes away . . .

GABE AND NATALIE:

For just another day.

(Lights. It's later.
In the bedroom, Dan holds Diana, after.)

DAN: That was great, wasn't it? It was great. Oh Christ, I'm late.
DIANA: That'll teach you to take a whole ten minutes.
DAN: Sorry, what?
DIANA: I said, isn't it a beautiful day?
DAN: Okay. Sure. I mean, it's cloudy, and raining, and really cold for September, but beautiful.
DIANA: Makes you want to dive in with both feet, doesn't it?
DAN: Absolutely.

(Diana goes. Dan speaks to us:)

I never know what she's talking about.

(He sings:)

When it's up to you to hold your house together . . .
A house you built with patience and with care . . .
But you're grappling with that gray and rainy weather,
And you're living on a latte and a prayer—

(Diana bustles in to the kitchen.)

DAN AND DIANA:

Can you keep the cup from tipping?
Can you keep your grip from slipping in despair?
For just another day

(Gabe is in his room, dressing for the day.)

DAN AND GABE:
In the hustle and the hurry

DAN:
You want to wipe your worry clean away.

DAN, GABE AND DIANA:
For just another day

DIANA:
I will keep the plates all spinning

DIANA AND NATALIE:
With a smile so white and winning all the way

DIANA, NATALIE, DAN AND GABE:
'Cause what doesn't kill me doesn't kill me,
So fill me up for just another day.

(Gabe sees Dan in the hall, and avoids him.)

GABE:
It only hurts when I'm here.

GABE, DIANA, NATALIE AND DAN:
Bum, Bum, Bum . . .

(Gabe joins Diana in the kitchen.)

DIANA: You're going to be late, and you've got a huge day.
GABE: You have no idea what I do all day.
DIANA: Jazz band before school, class, key club, then football.
GABE: Not bad.
DIANA: Now get out of here.

(As he goes, to us:)

It only hurts when he goes.

DIANA, GABE, NATALIE AND DAN:
> Bum, Bum, Bum . . .

(Gabe steps out of Natalie's way as she strides into the kitchen.)

GABE: Morning, sunshine.

(Natalie does not acknowledge him; she speaks to Diana:)

NATALIE: So I got the date for my winter recital—do you think you guys can come?
DIANA: We'll put it on the calendar.
NATALIE: Mom, the calendar is still on April of last year.
DIANA: Oh. Well, happy Easter!
NATALIE: Happy Easter, Mom.

(She goes, passing Dan as he enters.)

DAN: Hi, sweetheart.
NATALIE: She's on *fire* this morning.
DAN: Oh, I know.
NATALIE *(Oh, right)*: Eww.
DAN: Hon, can you do the shopping today? I'm slammed at work, and we're out of everything.
DIANA: I keep cave clean. You go out, get fire!
DAN: Uhh . . . absolutely.
> *(To us)* Again, no clue.

(He leaves the kitchen, gathering his briefcase, coat, portfolio.
> *Natalie and Gabe find backpacks and coats, tie shoes, get ready for the day.*
> *Diana pulls out the fixings for sandwiches, and starts making them on the table.)*

DIANA:
> It only hurts when I breathe.

DAN:
> It only hurts when I try.

GABE:

It only hurts when I think.

NATALIE:

It only hurts when I cry.

DAN:

It only hurts when I work.

GABE:

It only hurts when I play.

NATALIE:

It only hurts when I move.

DIANA:

It only hurts when I say . . .

(Diana's now making many sandwiches.)

NATALIE, GABE AND DAN:
It's just another day
And the morning sun is
    stunning
And you wish that you
Were running far away.
It's just another day—
Birds are singing, things
    are growing
And you wish you could
    be going
But you stay.
And you stay and stay
    forever,
Though you know it's
    now or never,
And you know that for
    forever . . .

DIANA:
A busy, busy day.

I will hold it all together.

I will hide the mess away.
And I'll survive another day
And I will pray

To hold on just this way

And for my fam'lys sake—
I'll take what I can take—

I'm only just awake . . .

DIANA:
Every day is just another
And another . . .
And another . . .

(Diana's now making way too many sandwiches, and just keeps making them.)

DIANA:
I will hold it all together
We're the perfect loving fam'ly
If they say we're not, then fuck 'em

DAN *(Going to her)*: Diana. Diana.

DIANA:
The perfect loving fam'ly
I will keep the plates all spinning
And the world just keeps on spinning
And I think the house is spinning . . .

(As Natalie and Gabe stand together, watching, Dan bends to her.)

DAN: Diana. Honey?
NATALIE: Dad?
DAN: Don't worry about it. Go on ahead. You'll miss the bus.
GABE: Mom?
DIANA: Everything's fine! I'm just making sandwiches. On the floor. You go on ahead. You'll miss the bus.
DAN *(To Natalie)*: Go.

(Natalie goes, and after a half beat, Gabe follows.)

Sweetie? Everything okay?
DIANA: I wanted to get ahead on lunches.
DAN: Sure. Let me help you up.
DIANA: I guess I got carried away.
DAN: Maybe a little. *(Helps her up)* Let's go see Doctor Fine. This is just a blip. Okay? Nothing to worry about. I'll wrap up the, um, sandwiches, and then we'll go.

(Lights. School bell.
Music.
Natalie is playing piano in a school practice room.)

everything else

NATALIE:
   Mozart was crazy.
   Flat fucking crazy.
   Batshit, I hear.

   But his music's not crazy.
   It's balanced, it's nimble,
   It's crystalline clear.

   There's harmony, logic—you listen to these,
   You don't hear his doubts or his debts or disease.
   You scan through the score and put fingers on keys
   And you play . . .
   And everything else goes away.
   Everything else goes away.

   And you play till it's perfect, you play till you ache,
   You play till the strings or your fingernails break.
   So you'll rock that recital and get into Yale,
   So you won't feel so sick and you won't look so pale,
   'Cause you've got your full ride and your early admit—
   So you're done with this school and with all of this shit
   And you graduate early, you're gone as of May
   And there's nothing your paranoid parents can say
   And you know that it's just a sonata away . . .
   And you play . . .
   And you play . . .
   And everything else goes away.

(Henry slips into the room, watching.)

   Everything else goes away.
   Everything else—

(Natalie sees Henry and stops.)

HENRY: Sounds good.
NATALIE: I still have this practice room for seven and a half minutes.
HENRY: Yeah, I mean, I know—I just like to listen. I'm Henry.
NATALIE: Natalie.
HENRY: Yeah. I mean, I know.
NATALIE: It's a little creepy that you know.
HENRY: We've gone to school together for, like, six years.
NATALIE: Really?
HENRY: I sit behind you in four classes.
NATALIE: Uh-huh. Also creepy.
HENRY: You're in here a lot. Before school, and after.
NATALIE: Right. Seven minutes.

(A brief moment, and Henry turns to go.)

You give up way too easily.

(Henry stops and turns back to her.)

HENRY: Uh. You're kind of a confusing person.
NATALIE: You should meet my mother.

*(She attacks the keys.
Music.
Lights.
Doctor Fine appears, in glasses, with clipboard, rumpled and world-weary. Diana listens.)*

DOCTOR FINE: The pink ones are taken with food but not with the white ones. The white ones are taken with the round yellow ones but not with the triangle yellow ones. The triangle yellow ones are taken with the oblong green ones with food but not with the pink ones. If a train is leaving New York at a hundred and twenty miles an hour and another train is leaving St. Petersburg at the same time but going backwards, which train . . .

(Dan walks back out to the car.
Doctor Fine fades as Dan sings:)

who's crazy / my psychopharmacologist and i

DAN:

Who's crazy? The husband or wife?
Who's crazy? To live their whole life
Believing that somehow
    things aren't as bizarre as they are?

Who's crazy—the one who can't cope,
Or maybe the one who'll still hope?
The one who sees doctors
    or the one who just waits in the car?

And I was
A wild twenty-five,
And I loved
A wife so alive,
But now I believe I would settle
For one who can drive.

DOCTOR FINE: The round blue ones with food but not with the
oblong white ones. The white ones with the round yellow
ones but not with the trapezoidal green ones. Split the green
ones into thirds with a tiny chisel.

(He continues, if necessary, until Diana interrupts:)

[Use a mortar and pestle to grind into a fine powder and
sprinkle the powder over a bowl of ice cream . . .]

(Diana sings as Doctor Fine silently continues his litany:)

DIANA:
My psychopharmacologist and I . . .
It's like an odd romance.
Intense and very intimate,
We do our dance.

My psychopharmacologist and I . . .
Call it a lover's game.
He knows my deepest secrets—
I know his . . . name.

And though he'll never hold me
He'll always take my calls.
It's truly like he told me:
Without a little lift,
The ballerina falls.

(Music changes to a jazz waltz.
In shadows, the voices [Natalie, Dan, Henry and Gabe] gather around, scatting.
Doctor Fine and Diana change positions: it's another week.)

DOCTOR FINE: Goodman, Diana. Bipolar depressive with delusional episodes. Sixteen-year history of medication. Adjustment after one week.
DIANA: I've got less anxiety, but I have headaches, blurry vision, and I can't feel my toes.
DOCTOR FINE: So we'll try again, and eventually we'll get it right.
DIANA: Not a very exact science, is it?

(Now the Voices sing a radio advertisement—perhaps with visual aids.)

VOICES:
Zoloft and Paxil and Buspar and Xanax . . .
Depakote, Klonopin, Ambien, Prozac . . .
Ativan calms me when I see the bills—
These are a few of my favorite pills.

(The Voices disappear.)

DIANA: Oh, thank you, Doctor. Valium is my favorite color. How'd you know?

(This time Henry is playing piano in the practice room, and Natalie joins him. He's playing the same jazz waltz we've been hearing.)

NATALIE: It's just that the thing with jazz is, how do you ever know if you got it right? It's just making shit up.
HENRY: Which is also known as the act of creation.
NATALIE: Oh. You're one of those pretentious stoner types.
HENRY: That's totally unfair. I'm not pretentious. And I'm definitely not classical. It's so rigid and structured. There's no room for improvisation. You have to play the notes on the page.
NATALIE: Yes, and what did Mozart know, anyway? He should have just smoked a bowl and jammed on "Twinkle, Twinkle Little Star."
HENRY: Yeah, let's do that!

(Doctor Fine is taking notes again.)

DOCTOR FINE: Goodman, Diana. Second adjustment after three weeks. Delusions less frequent but depressive state worse.
DIANA: I'm nauseous and I'm constipated. Completely lost my appetite and gained six pounds. Which, you know, is just not fair.

*(Doctor Fine and the Voices help Diana read the side-effects labels.
They pass many large pill bottles among them, slowly at first, then faster, then tossing, then juggling.)*

DOCTOR FINE AND VOICES:
    May cause the following side effects,
    One or more:

DOCTOR FINE: VOICES:
Dizziness, drowsiness,
Sexual dysfunction,
Headaches and tremors,   Diarrhea, constipation,
And nightmares and   Nervous laughter, palpitations,
seizures,

DIANA, DOCTOR FINE AND VOICES:
Anxiousness, anger,
Exhaustion, insomnia,
Irritability,
Nausea, vomiting,

DIANA:
Odd and alarming sexual feelings.

DIANA, DOCTOR FINE AND VOICES:
Oh, and one last thing—

(*All the bottles fall to the floor.*)

DOCTOR FINE:
Use may be fatal . . .

GABE:
Use may be fatal . . .

DAN:
Use may be fatal . . .

(*As if evading responsibility, the Voices wander away.*
Split scene:
Doctor Fine back with Diana.
While in the piano room, Henry and Natalie sit closer.)

DOCTOR FINE (*Writing*): Goodman, Diana. Third adjustment after five weeks. Reports continued mild anxiety and some lingering depression.

DIANA: I now can't feel my fingers or my toes. I sweat profusely for no reason.

NATALIE: I've wasted, like, weeks of practice with you in here. Improvising.

HENRY: Oscar Peterson was classically trained.

NATALIE: Beethoven did cocaine.

HENRY: Miles Davis went to Juilliard.

NATALIE: Mozart wrote poems about farts.

(Henry and Natalie are now very close . . .)

DIANA: Fortunately, I have absolutely no desire for sex. Although whether that's the medicine or the marriage is anybody's guess.

DOCTOR FINE: I'm sure it's the medicine.

DIANA *(Flattered)*: Oh, thank you, that's very sweet. But my husband's waiting in the car.

(. . . but instead of kissing, Henry and Natalie play furiously, four hands.
Lights on Dan, waiting in the car.)

DAN:

Who's crazy?
The one who's half-gone?
Or maybe
The one who holds on?
Remembering when she was twenty and brilliant and bold,
And I was so young and so dumb, and now I am . . . old.

DAN:	DIANA:
And she was	And though he'll never hold me,
Wicked and wired.	
The sex was	He'll always take my calls.
Simply inspired.	
Now there's no sex, she's depressed,	It's truly like he told me—
And me I'm just tired.	Without a little lift
Tired. tired. tired.	The ballerina falls.

DAN:	DIANA:
Who's crazy—	My psychopharmacologist and I,
The one who's uncured?	Together side by side . . .
Or maybe the one who's endured?	Without him
The one who has treatments, or the	I'd die . . .
One who just lives with the pain?	My psychopharmacologist and I.

(Diana is frozen in a waltz dip with Doctor Fine.
Gabe, Natalie and Henry disappear.
Dan is left alone again.)

DAN:

They say love is blind, but believe me—love is insane.

(Doctor Fine lifts Diana to her feet.
Dan leaves the car and goes to retrieve her.)

DOCTOR FINE: Goodman, Diana. Seven weeks.
DIANA: I don't feel like myself. I mean, I don't feel anything.
DOCTOR FINE *(Grunts, then writes)*: Hmpf. Patient stable.

(Lights.
Music.
Henry and Natalie in his bedroom. He's packing the bowl of a big-ass bong.)

NATALIE: Your mom is, like, in the next room.
HENRY: She's in denial—it's totally convenient.

(He takes a hit from the bong, then offers it. Natalie just looks at it, then him.)

Dude. It's therapeutic.
NATALIE: Right, it's medical marijuana to treat your ADD.

HENRY *(Takes another hit, then)*: Totally . . . huh?

NATALIE: I don't put anything into my mouth that's on fire.

HENRY: I guess that's a good rule.

(He goes to kiss her. She pulls away abruptly.)

NATALIE: Look. I can't do this. Not with my life. I'm like one fuck-up from disaster.

(Music changes.)

HENRY: Your life is not a disaster. The environment is a disaster. Sprint is a disaster.

NATALIE: You're stoned.

perfect for you

HENRY:

Our planet is poisoned, the oceans, the air,
Around and beneath and above you.

NATALIE:

Um, Henry, that's true, and I totally care—

HENRY:

I'm trying to tell you I love you.

NATALIE: What?

HENRY:

The world is at war, filled with death and disease—
We dance on the edge of destruction.
The globe's getting warmer by deadly degrees—

NATALIE:

And this is one fucked-up seduction.

HENRY:

> This planet is pretty much broken beyond all repair . . .
> But one thing is working
> If you're standing there.
>
> Perfect for you . . .
> I could be perfect for you.
> I might be lazy, a loner,
> A bit of a stoner—it's true.
> But I might be perfect—
> I'll make myself perfect . . .
> Perfect for you.

(As the music builds, Henry's bedroom goes away.)

> You square all the corners, I straighten the curves.

NATALIE:

> You've got some nerve, Henry, and I'm just all nerves.

HENRY:

> But even if everything else turns to dirt,

HENRY AND NATALIE:

> We'll be the one thing in this world that won't hurt.

HENRY:

> I can't fix what's fucked-up,
> But one thing I know I can do . . .
> I can be perfect for you.

NATALIE:

> I can be perfect for you.

NATALIE AND HENRY:

> Perfect for you.

> *(At last, they kiss.*
> *Lights.*

Music continues under.
They're on Natalie's front porch.)

HENRY: Nice house. Can I come in?
NATALIE: Oh my, no.
HENRY: Okay.

(They kiss again.
Diana is watching out a window. Gabe finds her and looks over her shoulder.)

GABE: Are you spying on your own daughter?
DIANA: When did she get a boyfriend? How did I miss this?
GABE: Well . . . you kind of miss a lot.
DIANA: Do you think they're in love?
GABE: Who knows? They're young, they're horny . . . it happens.

(Gabe goes. Dan appears, wearing a rugby shirt very much like the one Henry wears. It is years ago.)

DAN: Marry me.
DIANA: What?
DAN: Marry me. Let's have a family. I know, we're too young, but we're not, I'm almost twenty-two, and how do you know this isn't a sign saying we belong together?
DIANA: How do you know it's not a sign saying get new rubbers?
DAN: Because I know it's not. I love you, and this baby—
DIANA: Dan. This is crazy.
NATALIE *(Overlapping)*: This is crazy.
DAN AND HENRY: Maybe it is.

(Diana hears Henry and wakes from her reverie. She watches intently as Natalie and Henry kiss again.
Music changes.
Henry and Dan go.
Natalie hurries into the house, stops short when she sees Diana, and realizes she's been watching. Natalie looks stricken, then disappears into her room.
Diana watches her go.)

i miss the mountains

DIANA:

There was a time when I flew higher,
Was a time the wild girl running free
Would be me.
Now I see her feel the fire,
Now I know she needs me there to share—
I'm nowhere.

All these blank and tranquil years—
Seems they've dried up all my tears.
And while she runs free and fast,
Seems my wild days are past.

But I miss the mountains.
I miss the dizzy heights.
All the manic, magic days,
And the dark, depressing nights.

(She goes to her medicine cabinet and begins to take out a passel of pill bottles . . .)

I miss the mountains,
I miss the highs and lows,
All the climbing, all the falling,
All the while the wild wind blows,
Stinging you with snow
And soaking you with rain—
I miss the mountains,
I miss the pain.

(. . . and opens them . . .)

Mountains make you crazy—
Here it's safe and sound.
My mind is somewhere hazy—
My feet are on the ground.

Everything is balanced here
And on an even keel.
Everything is perfect—
Nothing's real . . .
Nothing's real.

(. . . and pours them in the toilet.)

And I miss the mountains.
I . . . I miss the lonely climb.
Wand'ring through the wilderness
And spending all my time
Where the air is clear
And cuts you like a knife—
I miss the mountains . . .
I miss the mountains . . .
I miss my life.
I miss my life.

(Music ends. Gabe enters.)

GABE: You sure about this, Mom?
DIANA: You think it's a bad idea.
GABE: I think it's a great idea. I think you're brave.
DIANA: What will your father think?
GABE: Nothing. If he doesn't know.

(He reaches out and gives the toilet a flush.
Lights, suddenly, and music.
Dan appears, joined by exuberant Voices.)

it's gonna be good

DAN AND VOICES:
It's gonna be good good good . . .
It's gonna be good good good . . .
It's gonna be good!
G . . . O . . . O . . . D good!

(Dan's at work.)

DAN:
>It's gonna be good!
>It's gonna be good.
>Two weeks and it's all working
>Just the way I knew it would—
>And I don't sit at work just waiting for the phone to ring!
>It's a good good good good thing.

(He stares at the phone a moment, and another moment, and then suddenly can't stand it any longer, grabs, and dials.)

VOICES:
>Ring! A-ling!
>Ring! A-ling!

(Diana, at home, is on the other end, as Dan fades.)

DIANA: Hello? Oh, hi! Everything's great here, sweetie. Fantastic. I disinfected the entire house, rewired the computer, and did some decoupage. Okay. Buh-bye.

(Hangs up the phone.)

Hmm. Next. I think I'll retile the roof!

(She goes, and Dan is in his car, on a different day.)

DAN:
>It's gonna be great!
>It's gonna be great.
>The sex is still amazing
>And we don't stay up that late.
>It's almost been a month and she's as happy as a clam . . .
>Do I look great? I am.

*(Music changes.
Lights.
Natalie and Henry are on her porch, again.)*

NATALIE: I'd ask you in, but it's too soon.
HENRY: We've been going out for nine weeks and three days. Don't I get to meet your family?
NATALIE: You keep count? You're so the girl. And no.

(But Dan emerges from inside and catches them, as Gabe watches.)

DAN: Natalie!

(Music changes.)

And this must be Harry!
GABE: It's Henry.
DAN: A pleasure to finally meet you. Come in. Why don't you join us for dinner?

(He puts his arm around Henry and ushers him in as Natalie follows.)

NATALIE: Um, Dad, Henry can't really stay. He's got, um . . .

DAN:
    It's gonna be good!

NATALIE: . . . homework.

DAN:
    It's gonna be good.

NATALIE: Surgery.

DAN:
    Gonna sit right down together
    Like a happy fam'ly should.

NATALIE: Rabies.

DAN:

And eat and talk and laugh and joke,
My pride, my brood, and me—
It's gonna be good,
You'll see.

(Without prompting, Gabe joins in happily:)

DAN AND GABE:

We'll smile and chat and just like that
We'll all be all okay . . .
It's gonna be great,
It's gonna be great,

*(Henry joins in cheerfully, and Natalie finally follows.
Diana serves and clears a full dinner in super-fast-motion. The
rest grab forkfuls where they can.)*

DAN, GABE, HENRY AND NATALIE:

It's gonna be gonna be gonna be great
That way . . .
Hey!
It's gonna be good!
It's gonna be good.
Gonna sit right down together
Like a happy fam'ly should.
And eat and talk and laugh and joke—
My family and me . . .
It's gonna be good gonna be good
Gonna be gonna be gonna be
Gonna be gonna be
Good good good good
Good good good good
Good good good good
Gonna be good gonna be good—
It's gonna be good you'll see.

*(Music ends. Diana enters with a birthday cake, blazing with candles.
But Gabe has disappeared.)*

DIANA: Okay . . . It's someone's birthday!
HENRY *(To Natalie)*: Whose birthday is it?
NATALIE *(Small pause)*: My brother's.
HENRY: I didn't know you had a brother.
NATALIE: I don't.

(Music.)

He died before I was born.
DIANA *(A beat, sees them)*: What? What is it?

(Dan goes to Diana.)

he's not here

DAN:

He's not here . . .
He's not here.
Love, I know you know.
Do you feel
He's still real?
Love, it's just not so.
Why is it you still believe?
Do you dream or do you grieve?
You've got to let him go.
He's been dead
All these years . . .
No, my love, he's not here.

NATALIE: This is fucked.
DAN: Language.
NATALIE: Fuck this.

(A beat, then Natalie storms out. Henry moves to follow, pausing for:)

HENRY: It was wonderful to meet you both.

(He goes. Dan goes to Diana.)

DAN: What about the new meds?
DIANA: We have the happiest septic tank on the block.
DAN: You—Jesus, Di. They were working.
DIANA: They weren't, really.
DAN: We'll get a new round, we'll call Doctor Fine—
DIANA: No.
DAN: Diana, look, I know this is hard.

(Music changes.)

DIANA: You know. Really? What, exactly, do you know?
DAN: I know you're hurting. I am, too.

you don't know

DIANA:
Do you wake up in the morning
And need help to lift your head?
Do you read obituaries
And feel jealous of the dead?
It's like living on a cliffside
Not knowing when you'll dive . . .
Do you know
Do you know what it's like to die alive?

When a world that once had color
    fades to white and gray and black . . .
When tomorrow terrifies you
    but you'll die if you look back.

You don't know.
I know you don't know.
You say that you're hurting—
It sure doesn't show.
You don't know . . .
It lays me so low

When you say let go
And I say
You don't know

The sensation that you're screaming
But you never make a sound,
Or the feeling that you're falling
But you never hit the ground—
It just keeps on rushing at you
Day by day by day by day . . .
You don't know
You don't know what it's like to live that way.

Like a refugee, a fugitive
    forever on the run . . .
If it gets me, it will kill me—
    but I don't know what I've done.

i am the one

DAN:

Can you tell me
What it is you're afraid of?
And can you tell me why I'm afraid it's me?
Can I touch you?
We've been fine for so long now,
How could something go wrong that I can't see?

'Cause I'm holding on,
And I won't let go
I just thought you should know . . .

I am the one who knows you,
I am the one who cares,
I am the one who's always been there.
I am the one who's helped you
And if you think that I just don't give a damn,
Then you just don't know who I am.

(Gabe appears, watching.)

DAN:	GABE:
Could you leave me?	Hey, Dad, it's me.
Could you let me go under?	Why can't you see?
Will you watch as I drown	
And wonder why?	I wonder why.

(Gabe steps between Dan and Diana, and speaks to Dan, who continues to sing to Diana. Gabe continues to try to get his attention.)

Are you bleeding?	Are you waiting, are you wishing,
	Are you wanting all that she can't give?
Are you bruised, are you broken?	Are you hurting, are you healing,
	Are you hoping for a life to live?
And does it help you to know	
That so am I?	Well, so am I.
Tell me what to do	Look at me.
Tell me who to be	Look at me.
So I can see what you see.	And you'll see . . .
I am the one who'll hold you	I am . . .
I am the one who'll stay	I am . . .
I am the one who won't walk away.	I won't walk away.
I am the one who'll hear you	I am . . .
And now you tell me that	
I won't give a damn	You don't give a damn.
But I know you know who I am.	Who I am
Yeah, yeah, yeah, yeah	Yeah, yeah, yeah, yeah
That's who I am (yeah yeah yeah yeah)	Who I am yeah, yeah, yeah, yeah

DAN:
 That's who I am (yeah
  yeah yeah yeah)
 That's who I am.

GABE:
Who I am yeah, yeah, yeah,
 yeah

DAN:
 'Cause I'm holding on . . .

DIANA:
 You say you hurt like me . . .

GABE:
 And I won't let go . . .

DIANA:
 You say that you know . . . oh . . .

DAN AND GABE:
 Yeah, I thought you should
  know.
 I am the one who knows you,
 I am the one who cares,
 I am the one who's always
  been there.
 Yeah, yeah, yeah
 I am the one who needs you
 And if you think that I just
 Don't give a damn
 Then you just don't know
  who I am
 Who I am
 Who I am

DIANA:
You don't know.
I know you don't know.
You say that you're hurting,
I know it ain't so.
You don't know . . .

Why don't you just go?
'Cause it lays me low
When I say
You don't know . . .

You don't know . . .
You don't know . . .

GABE:
 You just don't know who I am.

 (Lights.
  Music changes.
  Natalie is in her room with Henry. He is working on something
 at her desk.)

NATALIE: When she gets like this? She's useless. She can't use the phone. Can't drive.

HENRY: I bet she's got great pills. I mean, not that I would go there. That shit's inorganic.

NATALIE: And totally ineffective, apparently.

HENRY: I'm old-school. Dying breed. All the preppies and the jocks are raiding their parents' medicine cabinets and popping Xanax and snorting Adderall.

NATALIE: Really?

HENRY: But me, I'm the master of the lost art of making a pipe out of an apple.

(He proudly reveals his handiwork . . .)

NATALIE: Yeah, you're the MacGyver of pot.

(. . . and he offers it to her.)

You promise this'll help?

HENRY: No.

(She considers it, then turns away.)

What?

superboy and the invisible girl

NATALIE:
Superboy and the invisible girl . . .
Son of steel and daughter of air.
He's a hero, a lover, a prince—
She's not there.

Superboy and the invisible girl . . .
Everything a kid oughta be.
He's immortal, forever alive—
Then there's me.

I
Wish I could fly
And magically appear and disappear.

I
Wish I could fly—
I'd fly far away from here.

(Diana gently opens the door. Henry hides the pipe and fans the air, and Natalie whips around to confront her mother:)

Superboy and the invisible girl—
He's the one you wish would appear.
He's your hero, forever your son—
He's not here.
I am here.

DIANA:

You
Know that's not true.
You're our little pride and joy, our perfect plan.
You
Know I love you . . .
I love you as much as I can.

(A beat as this lands. Then, awkwardly, Diana leaves.)

NATALIE:

Take a look at the invisible girl . . .
Here she is, clear as the day.
Please look closely and find her before
She fades away.

(Through a wall, Gabe appears in Natalie's room. Natalie and Henry do not see him.)

NATALIE AND GABE:

Superboy and the invisible girl . . .
Son of steel and daughter of air.

He's a hero, a lover, a prince—
She's not there . . .
She's not there . . .

(She sits by Henry. He pulls the pipe out of hiding, and offers it.)

She's not there . . .
She's not there.

(She takes the pipe from Henry.
Music ends.
Lights.
Diana and Dan in a waiting room. Dan is writing in a notebook.)

DAN: Let's not get discouraged. We'll find a doctor who'll treat you without the drugs. There's someone out there for you— in the depression chat rooms, they say it's like dating, you have to keep going until you find the right match.
DIANA: They have depression chat rooms?
DAN: And this doctor's supposed to be fantastic. A real rock star. Three different women at work gave me his name.
DIANA: Three women at work know I'm nuts?
DAN *(Half beat)*: Uhh . . . *(Turns, looking for relief)* Ah!

(Doctor Madden appears.)

DOCTOR MADDEN: Diana? This way, please.

(She walks past him into his inner office, studying him. Once she's past him—music, a chord, lights hit—and he's briefly a rock star.)

Yeah . . .

DIANA *(Spins around; lights restore)*: What did you just say?
DOCTOR MADDEN *(A doctor again)*: I said welcome. Have a seat. It's nice to meet you.

(Watching him suspiciously, she sits, turns, and—another chord—he's a rock star again:)

Let's get it on now, baby . . .

DIANA: Excuse me, what?

DOCTOR MADDEN *(Now not a rock star)*: I said, let's get started. Are you . . . nervous, Diana?

DIANA: I am, a little. A bit out of breath. Tingly, actually. *(He nods, waits)* Now you go.

DOCTOR MADDEN: Well, let's start by getting to know each other a bit. Psychotherapy and medication work best in tandem, but we can try the first alone, and see how far we get. Why don't you tell me—

(A sudden chord—and he's a rock star again:)

Bay-bee . . . what's your history?
Where'd you go and who'd you see? Yeah . . .

(And just like that he's not a rock star.)

DIANA: Um. My history?

(He nods mildly.)

Well—I was diagnosed bipolar, um, wow, sixteen years ago? But it turned out bipolar didn't totally cover it.

DOCTOR MADDEN: Often the best we can do is put names on collections of symptoms. It's possible bipolar has more in common with schizophrenia than depression.

DIANA: When I was young, my mother called me "high-spirited." She would know. She was so high-spirited they banned her from the PTA.

DOCTOR MADDEN: Sometimes there's a predisposition to illness, but actual onset is only triggered by some . . . traumatic event.

DIANA: I never know what to say when I have to go over all this. It starts to sound like some story I tell that's about some other person entirely.

DOCTOR MADDEN: Why don't you tell me about the last time you truly felt happy.

(She has no answer for him.)

Were you happy when you got married?
DIANA: I thought I was.
DOCTOR MADDEN: There's a difference between being happy and just thinking you're happy?
DIANA: Most people who think they're happy just haven't thought about it enough. Most people who think they're happy are actually just stupid.
DOCTOR MADDEN: I see. Were you happy when your son was born?

(Music changes.)

DIANA: My son?

(Gabe appears, watching.)

DOCTOR MADDEN: Tell me about him.
DIANA: About my son?
DOCTOR MADDEN: Why is he still around? Who is he? What is he?

(Diana does not answer. Gabe sings:)

i'm alive

GABE:
I am what you want me to be,
And I'm your worst fear—you'll find it in me.
Come closer . . .
Come closer . . .

DOCTOR MADDEN: Where does he come from, do you think?

(Doctor Madden and Diana sit in silence . . .)

GABE:

> I am more than memory—
> I am what might be, I am mystery.
> You know me—
> So show me.

(. . . as Gabe circles them.)

> When I appear it's
> Not so clear if
> I'm a simple spirit or I'm flesh and blood . . .

(Now rock star lights hit him and he sings to us:)

> But I'm alive
> I'm alive
> I am so alive,
> And I feed on the fear that's behind your eyes.

> And I need you
> To need me
> It's no surprise—
> I'm alive . . .
> So alive . . .
> I'm alive.

(Natalie, with backpack, has just arrived home from school.)

NATALIE: Four times a week? That's a lot, isn't it?

DAN: It's what the doctor recommended.

NATALIE *(After a pause)*: This is never going to get better, is it?

(Gabe joins them, listening.)

> He's never going away.

DAN: I don't know, Natalie.

NATALIE: This is one of those moments when you could just be a typical parent and lie and say yes.

DAN: Yes.

NATALIE: Thanks. That's comforting.

(Dan is silent at first, and Natalie turns to go . . .)

GABE:

I am flame and I am fire,
I am destruction, decay, and desire—
I'll hurt you . . .

(. . . but Dan follows her with:)

DAN: You know, Natalie . . .

GABE:

I'll heal you . . .

DAN: It's not all about your comfort.

GABE:

I'm your wish, your dream come true,
And I am your darkest nightmare, too—
I've shown you . . .

DAN: It's about helping your mother.

GABE:

I own you.

NATALIE: As always.

(She goes. Gabe turns to Dan.)

GABE:

And though you made me,
You can't change me—
I'm the perfect stranger who knows you too well.

And I'm alive
I'm alive

I am so alive,
And I'll tell you the truth if you let me try.

You're alive
I'm alive
And I'll show you why
I'm alive . . .
So alive . . .
I'm alive.

(Gabe finds Natalie in the bathroom. He opens the medicine cabinet for her. She looks inside, and pulls out a pill bottle.)

NATALIE: Risperdal?

GABE:

> I'm alive . . .

NATALIE *(More bottles)*: Valium? Xanax?

GABE:

> I'm alive . . .

NATALIE *(Shrugs)*: What the hell.

*(She pours out a couple pills and pops them.
Gabe leaves her and returns to Doctor Madden's office . . .)*

GABE:

> I'm alive—I'm right behind you.
> You say forget, but I remind you.
> You can try to hide, you know that I will find you.
> 'Cause if you won't grieve me
> You won't leave me behind . . .

(. . . where Diana is still silent.)

DOCTOR MADDEN: Let's say he's eighteen now—isn't that when kids move out? Isn't it time to let him go?

GABE:
No, no, no—
I'm alive
I'm alive
I am so alive,
If you climb on my back, then we both can fly

If you try
To deny me
I'll never die
I'm alive . . .
So alive . . .
I'm alive . . .
Yeah, yeah . . .
I'm alive . . .
I'm alive . . .
I'm alive . . .
I'm alive!

(Music ends.
Diana sits opposite Doctor Madden again. Silence, then:)

DOCTOR MADDEN: It's been four weeks, and I'd like to try something new today. Sometimes, when these stories are hard to tell, hypnosis can be helpful.

(Music.)

DIANA: Oh, I don't think I could be hypnotized. I mean, it's fine. I'm just not the type.
DOCTOR MADDEN: Put your feet on the floor. Your hands in your lap. Breathe.

(She does. He sings:)

make up your mind / catch me i'm falling

Walk with me . . .
Walk with me.

DIANA: Okay. Walking.

DOCTOR MADDEN:
    Go all the way down—down a long flight of stairs . . .

DIANA: Stairs!

DOCTOR MADDEN:
    Go step by step into the darkness down there.

DIANA: Should we turn on a light? You know, with the stairs?

DOCTOR MADDEN (*Breathes, then*):
    Walk with me . . .
    Down a hall,
    A hall that you know—at the end, there's a door,
    It's a door that you've never laid eyes on before . . .
    Open the door . . .
    Open the door.

    (*Diana is silent. He speaks:*)

    Can you hear me, Diana?
DIANA: Yes.
DOCTOR MADDEN: Are you nervous?
DIANA: No.
DOCTOR MADDEN: Good. Now.

    (*Sings:*)

    Make up your mind to explore yourself.
    Make up your mind you have stories to tell.
    We'll search in your past
    For what sorrows may last,
    Then make up your mind to be well.

    (*Dan appears.*)

DAN: Di, you come home from these sessions in tears. Is this help-
    ing, or . . . ? Di? Di?

(Lights.
Another session. Diana is again hypnotized.)

DIANA: We were both undergrads. Architecture. The baby wasn't planned. Neither was the marriage. I had always expected to be too busy. But when the baby came it all seemed to make sense. Until . . . Until . . .

DOCTOR MADDEN: Until?

DAN AND VOICES:
> He's not here . . .
> He's not here . . .
> Love, I know you know.

DOCTOR MADDEN:
> Make up your mind that you're strong enough.
> Make up your mind—let the truth be revealed.
> Admit what you've lost
> And live with the cost . . .
> At times it does hurt to be healed.

(Gabe approaches, watching.)

GABE:
> Catch me I'm falling . . .

DOCTOR MADDEN: In our first session you told me . . .

GABE:
> Catch me I'm falling . . .

DOCTOR MADDEN: . . . that talking through your history . . .

GABE:
> Faster than anyone should.

GABE AND DIANA:
> Catch me I'm falling . . .

DOCTOR MADDEN: . . . it feels like it's about someone else.

GABE AND DIANA:
   Please hear me calling . . .

DOCTOR MADDEN: Make it about you.

GABE AND DIANA:
   Catch me I'm falling for good.

(Lights.
Backstage at the school auditorium.
Natalie fidgets. Henry enters, with flowers.)

HENRY: Hey. I'm not supposed to be backstage, but . . .

(He hands her the flowers.)

   For luck.
NATALIE: Did you see my parents out there?
HENRY: Um—are you okay?
NATALIE: I'm fine. My dad said they'd both be here.
HENRY: Then I'm sure they will be.
NATALIE: Will they?

(At the recital, over Diana's speech, Natalie steps out onstage and
peers at the audience—she does not see her parents.)

DIANA: We had Natalie to . . . And I know she knows. I couldn't
   hold her, in the hospital?
NATALIE: Where the hell are they?
DIANA: I couldn't let myself hold her.
DOCTOR MADDEN: That's the first time you've mentioned Natalie
   in weeks of therapy.
NATALIE: God*damn* it.

NATALIE AND VOICES:
      She's not there . . .
      She's not there . . .
      She's not there.

DOCTOR MADDEN:
Make up your mind you want clarity:
Take what you know and then make it make sense.
Just face what you fear,
And soon it comes clear
The visions are just your defense.

(Natalie shakily takes the stage at her recital. She looks out at the audience. Takes a deep breath.)

NATALIE: Um. Thank you for coming. Natalie Goodman.

(She sits at the piano, and tries to play the first bars of her piece— mangling it badly.)

DOCTOR MADDEN: Let's try to understand what all this is doing to you. And your family.

(Natalie tries a second time—disaster.)

NATALIE: Fuck.
DOCTOR MADDEN: Your grief for your son. Your distance from Natalie.

(As Henry peeks out from the wings, Natalie turns to the audience:)

NATALIE: I'm sorry. I just— The thing is—I—

(Music.)

You know what the problem with classical is? It's so rigid and structured. You have to play the notes on the page. There's no room for improvisation.
HENRY: Oh no.

(Natalie launches into a slightly sloppy but rousing rock riff which leads to:)

DOCTOR MADDEN:	DIANA:	DAN:	GABE:	NATALIE AND HENRY:
	Catch me		I'm alive . . .	
Make up	I'm fal-			Take a look...
your mind	ling . . .	He's not here.	I'm	Take a look...
You can live	Falling . . .		Alive . . .	
at last.			A-	The invisible
Make up				girl,
your mind	Fal-	Love,	live . . .	
To be fully	ling . . .			
alive.				
Embrace		It's	A-	fal-
what's inside,				
Replace what				
has died				
Then make				
up your mind				
you'll survive.		Time to go.	live . . .	ling . . .

DIANA, DAN, GABE AND NATALIE:
    Catch me I'm falling . . .

DOCTOR MADDEN: Unresolved loss can lead to depression.

DIANA, DAN, GABE AND NATALIE:
    Catch me I'm falling . . .

(Henry goes to Natalie . . .)

DOCTOR MADDEN: Fear of loss, to anxiety.

DIANA, DAN, GABE AND NATALIE:
    Flying headfirst into fate.
    Catch me I'm falling . . .

(. . . and tries to help her up from the piano.)

DOCTOR MADDEN: The more you hold on to something you lost . . .

DIANA, DAN, GABE AND NATALIE:
Please hear me calling . . .

(She resists at first . . .)

DOCTOR MADDEN: . . . the more you fear losing it

DIANA, DAN, GABE AND NATALIE:
Catch me before it's too late.

(. . . but finally lets him help her up. She holds on to him to keep from falling.)

DOCTOR MADDEN:	DAN, GABE AND NATALIE:
Depression, anxiety, depression, anxiety . . . One gives rise to the other.	Catch me before it's too late. Catch me before it's too late. Catch me I'm falling . . . Catch me I'm falling . . . Catch me I'm falling . . .

DOCTOR MADDEN: Wouldn't you like to be free from all that? Finally? Wouldn't you like to go home, clear out his room . . . maybe spend some time with your daughter? And let your son go, at last?
HENRY: Uh. Should we go?
NATALIE: Yes.
DIANA: Yes.
GABE: Mom.
DIANA: Yes I would.

*(Music.
The others disappear. Doctor Madden's office goes away.
Diana is at home.
Dan brings her a box of items from the baby's room.)*

DAN: This is good, Di. It's a good step.

(He goes.
Diana sifts through the items. She takes out Gabe's blanket, unfolds
it, holds it, folds it again, then drapes it on the arm of the chair.
She lifts a music box. She considers it a long moment, then opens
it. Music changes.)

i dreamed a dance

DIANA:

> I saw you light the ballroom
> With your sparkling eyes of blue.
> Graceful as an angel's wing,
> I dreamed a dance with you.

(Gabe enters, dressed stunningly in a tuxedo . . .)

> You whispered slyly, softly.
> You told me you would be true.
> We spun around a thousand stars—
> I dreamed a dance with you.

(. . . and they dance, beautifully.)

> I know the night is dying, dear . . .
> I know the day will dawn . . .

DIANA AND GABE:

> The dancers may disappear—
> Still the dance goes on . . .

GABE:

> And on.

(Gabe kisses her hand and steps away.)

DIANA:

> I'll wake alone tomorrow,
> The dream of our dances through.

But now until forever, love
I'll live to dance with you.

(Gabe turns to go . . .)

I'll dream, my love . . .
I'll live, my love . . .
And I'll die to dance with—

*(. . . but on this last, he turns back to her, and she falls silent.
Music changes.)*

there's a world

GABE:

There's a world . . .
There's a world I know.
A place we can go
Where the pain will go away—
There's a world where the sun shines each day.

There's a world . . .
There's a world out there.
I'll show you just where,
And in time I know you'll see
There's a world where we can be free—
Come with me.

(Doctor Madden enters with a hospital chart.)

DOCTOR MADDEN: Goodman, Diana.

GABE:

Come with me.

DOCTOR MADDEN: Discovered unconscious at home.

GABE:

There's a world where we can be free . . .

DOCTOR MADDEN: Multiple razor wounds to wrists and forearms. Self-inflicted.

GABE:

Come with me.

DOCTOR MADDEN: Saline rinse, sutures and gauze. IV antibiotics. Isolated, sedated and restrained. Damn it . . .

(Gabe holds out his hand. A moment, then Diana takes it, and follows him off.
Music changes.)

ECT is indicated.

(Dan joins him at the hospital.)

DAN: Wow. I mean—they still do that?
DOCTOR MADDEN: We do, yes. It's the standard in cases like this. She's got a long history of drug therapy and resistance, she's acutely suicidal—it's really our best option.
DAN: That's kind of terrifying.
DOCTOR MADDEN: It's not. The electricity involved is barely enough to light a hundred-watt bulb.
DAN *(Wry)*: Oh, if it's just a hundred-watt bulb . . .
DOCTOR MADDEN: It's safer than crossing the street, and the short-term success rate is over eighty percent.
DAN: I thought she was better . . .
DOCTOR MADDEN: Sometimes patients recover just enough strength to follow through on suicidal impulses, but not enough strength to resist them.
DAN: Well, that seems very . . . fucked.
DOCTOR MADDEN: Yes. *(Hands Dan a clipboard)* Legally, we need her consent. Hospital policy is we need yours, too.
DAN: I don't think she's gonna go for this.
DOCTOR MADDEN: Mister Goodman, we can administer the ECT and you can bring her home in ten days. Or we can keep her sedated for forty-eight hours, then discharge her and wait for her to try again. Look—go home. Take the night. We'll talk to her in the morning.

(Music changes.
Doctor Madden goes.
Dan is at home.)

i've been

DAN:

Standing in this room,
Well, I wonder what comes now.
I know I have to help her—
But hell if I know how.

And all the times that I've been told
The way her illness goes—
The truth of it is no one really knows.

And every day this act we act gets more and more
     absurd . . .
And all my fears just sit inside me, screaming to be
     heard . . .
I know they won't, though—not a single word.

(Dan starts to clean up after Diana.
Gabe appears and watches him.)

I was here,
At her side,
When she called,
When she cried . . .
How could she leave me on my own?

Will it work?
This cure?
There's no way
To be sure . . .
But I'm weary to the bone.

And whenever she goes flying
I keep my feet right on the ground—
Oh, now I need a lift and there's no one around.

*(As Dan finishes cleaning, he and Gabe both sing without words.
Then:)*

And I've never had to face the world
    without her at my side . . .
Now I'm strolling right beside her
    as the black hole opens wide . . .
Mine is just a slower suicide.

I've been here,
For the show,
Every high,
Every low . . .
But it's the worst we've ever known.

She's been hurt,
And how,
But I can't
Give up now
'Cause I've never been alone . . .
I could never be alone.

(Natalie enters.)

NATALIE: Dad. Why didn't you take me with you?

(Music changes.)

DAN: We don't see much of you these days. Is this Henry a good
    influence?
NATALIE: Like, compared to what?
DAN *(Beat)*: Okay, that's fair.

*(Split scene:
    Lights on Diana, in a bathrobe, with Doctor Madden at the hos-
pital. Gabe looks on.)*

DOCTOR MADDEN: The aftereffects are minimal. You'll feel a bit like you have a hangover.

GABE: Mom, don't let them do this. It causes brain damage.

DAN: Your mother's in for a new treatment. ECT.

NATALIE: Okay—L-M-N-O-P—what is that? I don't know.

DAN: Electroconvulsive therapy. Shock therapy.

DOCTOR MADDEN: A minority of patients report some memory loss, but it's usually not much memory.

GABE: How do you know how much memory you've lost if you've lost it?

NATALIE: You're kidding, right? Dad! That's bullshit.

(Music changes.)

DAN: Language.

DOCTOR MADDEN: Patients have said it's like becoming a new person.

NATALIE: It's bullshit. She trusts you.

(Natalie turns and runs off, and Dan follows.)

DAN: Natalie!

didn't i see this movie?

DIANA:
Didn't I see this movie,
With McMurphy and the nurse?
That hospital was heavy
But this cuckoo's nest is worse.
And isn't this the one where
In the end the good guys fry?
Didn't I see this movie
And didn't I cry?
Didn't I cry?

DOCTOR MADDEN: The modern procedure's clean and simple. Hundreds of thousands of patients receive it every year.

DIANA:

What makes you think I'd lose my mind for you?
I'm no sociopath.
I'm no Sylvia Plath.
I ain't no Frances Farmer kind of find for you . . .
So stay out of my brain—
I'm no princess of pain.

Didn't I see this movie
Where the doctor looked like you?
Where the patient got impatient
And said, "Sorry, Doc, I'm through.
I know where this is going,

And I know what you're about—
'Cause I have seen this movie
And I walked out."
I walked out.
I'm walking—

(Dan enters. He nods to Doctor Madden, who goes. Music changes.)

a light in the dark

DAN:

One light shines in the drive—
One single sign that our house is alive.
Our house, our own—
So why do I live there alone?

Tell me why I wait through the night,
And why do I leave on the light?
You know. I know.
Our house was a home long ago.

Take this chance,
'Cause it may be our last

To be free,
To let go of the past,
And to try,
To be husband and wife
To let love never die—
Or to just live our life.

Take my hand,
And let me take your heart,
Keep it far
From what keeps us apart—
Let us start
With a light in the dark.

DAN: DIANA:

Night falls, I stare at the walls. I stare at these walls . . .
I wake and wander the halls.   I get lost in these halls . . .
And I ache to the bone . . .

                             It's like nothing I've known . . .
I can't get through this alone. I can't get through this alone.

DAN:

Take this chance
And we'll make a new start
Somewhere far
From what keeps us apart,
And I swear that somewhere in the night
There's a light . . .
A light in the dark.

(Dan hands her the consent form and she signs it. Doctor Madden enters. So does Gabe.
Diana hands the clipboard back to Dan. Doctor Madden gestures to Diana, she stands, and follows him. Dan and Gabe watch.
Diana stops and turns for one last look at Dan.
Lights.)

act two

In black: music.
Natalie is with Henry outside a club.

NATALIE: Come ON. This is my favorite club. Let's go in.
HENRY: Isn't three clubs a little much for a Tuesday night? *(Checks his cell)* Wednesday morning?
NATALIE: Oh, come on. They're playing my favorite song.
HENRY: They're all your favorite song. What are you on?
NATALIE: Adderall. Xanax. And Valium. And Robitussin.
HENRY: When did *you* become a bad influence on *me?*
NATALIE: Hey, I am under *stress.* My mom is in a hospital being electrocuted.

(Natalie goes into the club. Henry follows.
Split scene:
At the hospital, the patient in headcap and gown is rolled in on a gurney. A Nurse and a Doctor [Dan and Gabe], in gowns and masks, assist Doctor Madden.)

DOCTOR MADDEN: Good morning, Diana. It's good to see you.
NATALIE *(Shouting over the music)*: Seriously—she gets it like every day for two weeks. I can't even deal. I'd never let them fuck with my brain like that.

(She pops a pill and downs it with Red Bull.)

HENRY *(Also shouting)*: No, you're strictly a do-it-yourself-er.

(Doctor Madden leans in to the patient as the others prepare for the procedure.)

DOCTOR MADDEN: I see you've met our anesthesiologist. Now, just breathe normally. Relax. Count backward from one hundred, and before you reach one, you'll be asleep. *(His voice begins to distort)* When you wake up, you may feel some muscle stiffness, disorientation—don't worry. It's completely normal. Diana? Diana? Good.

(He gently places the electrodes against her temples, and suddenly: Music.
Lights change . . .)

wish i were here

(. . . and suddenly Diana appears, watching herself on the table.)

DIANA:
In an instant, lightning flashes
And the burst might leave me blind—
When the bolt of lightning crashes
And it burns right through my mind.

It's like someone drained my brain out,
Set my frozen mind to thaw.
Let the lethargy and pain out
While I stood and watched, in awe.

I am riding on the brightest buzz . . .
I am worlds away from who I was . . .
And they told me it would change me—
Though they don't know how it does.

I have lived a life of clouds and gray,
But this is crystal clear . . .
Wish I were here.

I imagine it's remarkable.
Exuberant. Austere.
Wish I were here.
Wish I were here.

NATALIE:

It's euphoria, it's anger.
It's the winter wind, it's fire.
And it kills my deepest hunger
As it fills me with desire.

NATALIE WITH DIANA'S ECHO:

I'm the light and heat of ev'ry sun . . .
I'm a bullet from a magic gun . . .
And I'm trying to enjoy it—
But I'm missing all the fun.

Am I feeling what I think I'm feeling?
The hope, the heat, the fear?
Wish I were here.

Is this someone else's head trip?
Do I just disappear?

NATALIE AND DIANA:

Wish I were here.
Wish I were here.

(Diana joins Natalie, in the ether.)

DIANA: Sweetheart! What are you doing in my electricity?
NATALIE: It's always about you, isn't it? I'm Robotripping. I can't feel my legs.
DIANA: I don't want you doing drugs.

NATALIE: That's persuasive, coming from the Pfizer Woman of the Year. You're the one who's hallucinating.

DIANA: It's my treatment. It's a miracle. Everything is different now.

NATALIE: I know what you mean.

NATALIE AND DIANA:
Plug me in
And turn me on
And flip the switch—
I'm good as gone.

It slips my skin
And trips my brain—
I feel the burn
But I don't feel the pain.

Is my brain reborn or is it wrecked?
In freedom or in fear?
Wish I were here.

Have I blown my mind forever?
Is cloudy my new clear?
Wish I were here.
Wish I were here.
Wish I were—

*(In the hospital, the gurney and nurses go.
In the club, Natalie collapses.)*

HENRY: Natalie! Natalie! Damn.

(He helps her stand and leave the club.)

This is like the fifth night in a row I've had to come find you at some random club.

(Dan enters the hospital room, where Diana waits, dressed to go home.)

DAN: Diana?

(She looks at him a moment, makes a great effort, then:)

DIANA: Dan.
DAN: Your two weeks are up—time to go home!
DIANA: Home? But—

(Music changes.)

DAN: Shh. Don't talk. Relax.

> *(He puts a sweater around her shoulders and takes her bag. They go.
> Lights change. Natalie and Henry, at home, her dress rumpled
> from the night.)*

NATALIE: Okay. You can go. I'm, like, seventy percent less messed
up now.

> *(He doesn't go.)*

Seriously, my dad's gonna be home any minute. He's bring-
ing my mom from the hospital this morning, and you don't
want to be here.
HENRY: Will you call me?
NATALIE: Just go!

> *(Finally, he does.)*

> Can I hide my stupid hunger?
> Fake some confidence and cheer?
> Wish I were here.
> Wish I were here.

> *(Dan leads Diana gently into the house. She stops and takes it
> all in.)*

DAN: We're here.

(Natalie hurriedly does her dress up and smoothes it, trying to look nice. She hurries to join them, stopping short at the sight of Diana.)

NATALIE: Hey. Wow. Uh. You look . . . great.
DIANA: Oh, well, thank you. And who are you?
NATALIE: Who am I?
DAN: Diana. This is Natalie.
NATALIE: Your *daughter?*
DIANA: Oh. Of course. And this is our house?
DAN: Diana, don't you . . .

(Music.)

. . . You don't remember . . . any of this?
DIANA: I should, right?

song of forgetting

DAN:

This house and all these rooms?
Last Christmas or last year?
Out back the dogwood blooms—

DIANA:

Do I really live here?

DAN:

The paint, the walls . . .
All this glass and wood . . .
You don't recall?

DIANA:

How I wish I could.

DAN:

Our house on Walton Way—
The house with the red door?
Our trip to Saint-Tropez—
The whole week a downpour?

NATALIE:

    My first few steps . . .
And my first lost tooth . . .
What, nothing yet?

DIANA:

    To tell the truth . . .

NATALIE: Jesus.

DAN:

    Sing a song of forgetting . . .
A song of the way things were not.
Sing of what's lost to you,
Of times that you never knew . . .

    Sing of not remembering when,
Of mem'ries that go unremembered, and then
Sing a song of forgetting again.

    That day our child was born—
Our baby girl's first cry?
That gray and drizzly morn—
I've never felt so high.

DIANA:

    The day we met . . .
And we shared two beers . . .

DAN:

    Then?

DIANA:

    I forget.

DAN:

    But that's nineteen years.

DIANA: That Doctor Mitchell said there might be some memory
    loss.

DAN: Doctor Madden.

DIANA: Well, see, there you go.

NATALIE:

> What a lovely cure . . .
> It's a medical miracle.
> With a mind so pure
> That she doesn't know anything.

DAN:

> It's there I'm sure—
> 'Cause memories don't die.

NATALIE:

> Why?

DAN:

> They don't die.

NATALIE:

> They die . . .

DIANA:

> I'll try . . .

DIANA, NATALIE AND DAN:

> Sing a song of forgetting . . .
> A song of the way things were not.
> Sing of what's lost to you,
> Of times that you never knew.
> Sing of not remembering when . . .
> Of memories that go unremembered, and then
> Sing a song of forgetting again.

> *(A school bell.*
> *Lights.*
> *Dan helps Diana off.*
> *Music.*
> *Natalie grabs her backpack and leaves the house. Henry meets*
> *her, also with backpack. They're at school.)*

hey #1

HENRY:

Hey.

NATALIE:

Hey.

HENRY:

I've missed you these days.
I thought you might call—
It's been weeks.

NATALIE:

I've been crazed.

HENRY:

Hey . . .

Hey . . .
Have you been on the scene?
'Cause you look like a mess.

NATALIE:

Thanks, I guess.

HENRY:

Are you clean?

NATALIE:	HENRY:
Wow—coming from you—	
	I don't do what you do.
Okay, how did it start?	
	But you took it too far.
Oh, I took it too far?	
	Hey—hey—
Henry don't—	
	Are we over?

NATALIE: HENRY:
  Don't do this to me

                           Don't say that we're over . . .

  Don't you want us to be?

                           No—I want who I knew . . .
                           She's somewhere in you.

(Natalie moves away from him. He follows.)

HENRY:
    Hey.
    Say,
    Will you come to this dance?
    It's some spring formal dance.
    It's March first.
    And it's cheese.
    But it's fun and it's free—

(He holds up a pair of tickets.)

NATALIE:
    I don't do dances.

HENRY:
    Do this dance, with me.

NATALIE:
    Good-bye, Henry.

(She goes.)

HENRY: Natalie. Natalie, wait up.

(He chases after her.
Lights.
Music changes.
Diana and Dan are with Doctor Madden in his office.)

DOCTOR MADDEN: This much loss is rare, but it has been reported.
It may be partly psychogenic—at times like this the mind

tends to repress troubling memories. But they're still there, somewhere. They tend to return in fits and starts.

DAN: It's been two weeks.

seconds and years

DOCTOR MADDEN:

A little loss of memory is normal,
And helpful in forgetting all her fears.

DAN:

I couldn't give a flying fuck what's normal—
We haven't had a normal day in years.

DOCTOR MADDEN: Diana.

Are things becoming clearer with the treatment?

DIANA: Well, yes.

DOCTOR MADDEN:
Is life less cloudy than it was before?

DIANA: Yes.

DOCTOR MADDEN:
Do you still feel your head is filled with concrete?

DIANA: No.

And you're not a scary rock star anymore.

DOCTOR MADDEN *(Beat)*: Okay. Great.

DAN: But what about her memory?

(Music changes. As Diana goes, Doctor Madden takes Dan aside.)

better than before

DOCTOR MADDEN:

The memories are there, somewhere.
Find some pictures you can share,
Keepsakes of the life that's there behind her.

DAN: Should I bring up the subject of, um . . .
DOCTOR MADDEN: Yes . . .

But keep it light at first, that's best.
Careful that she's not distressed.
When the time's right, tell the rest . . . remind her.
You'll find her.

(Dan goes to Diana and Natalie in the kitchen, a box of photos and keepsakes before them.)

DAN:

So let's start with something small,
Something personal and pretty . . .
I bet you'll know these shiny things.

DIANA *(Spoken in time)*: They must be tacky trinkets from, I guess, Atlantic City?

DAN:

No, actu'ally, Di, they're our wedding rings.

NATALIE: It's going well.

DAN:

Here's a flower from our wedding,
It was such a sight to see—
With the ceremony everything we'd hoped.

NATALIE: Um, Dad?

DAN *(To Natalie)*:

Well, that's how I remember it, so that's how it'll be.

NATALIE:

It was raining, it was Portland, you eloped.

I mean, Portland?

DAN:

It's an open book to write here,
It's a life we can restore.
We can get back what we had and maybe more . . .
Maybe get us back to better than before.

NATALIE: You're missing a few pictures here, aren't you, Dad?
Didn't the doctor say—
DAN: The doctor said at the right time.
NATALIE: Oh, well then.

DAN:

Here's the year we drove the West,
We hit the highway in the Honda,
And I took pictures everywhere we went.

(Hands Diana three pictures, in sequence:)

We saw the painted desert, the Grand Canyon, and Aunt
Rhonda,

(Another picture:)

And Nat learned what her middle finger meant.

(Another batch:)

Here's the first house that we owned,
On Walton Way, we loved that place.
Then we built this one on land that we both chose.
And here's a pic of all of us with smiles on ev'ry face . . .
And the Photoshopping hardly even shows.

DIANA:

We're standing by a lake with all these ducks . . .
And who's this little chubby girl?

DAN:

That's Natalie.

NATALIE:

This sucks.

(She starts to leave, but Dan moves to stop her.)

DAN: Hey. Nat.

Gonna get us back to normal
Gonna get us back to good . . .
Gonna get back what we had and maybe more.

Gonna get us back to good times
And forget the things we should.
Gonna get us back to better than before . . .
We can get things back to better than before.

NATALIE: All right. Fine.

(Lifts a different stack of photos:)

Here's the headline in the paper
When you freaked out at the market.
Here's the house on Walton Way after the fire.

DAN: Natalie.

NATALIE:

Here's the damage to the Honda
When you showed me how to park it.

DIANA *(Takes picture, studies it):*
Did we crush somebody's cat beneath the tire?

NATALIE: Yes. Ours.

(More pictures:)

> Here's Dad at my recital,
> And we're wond'ring where you are.

DIANA:

> I remember this—I made it to the school.

DAN: Wait, you remember?

DIANA:

> It was the year of too much lithium—
> I hid out in the car.

(Another picture:)

> And your swim meet—just last year—
> I'm in the pool.

NATALIE: So you are.

DAN:

> You're getting it! You've got it, Di! Hooray!

DIANA *(To Natalie)*:
> Your life has kind of sucked, I think.

NATALIE:
> You got it! Yay! Hooray!

DAN:
> Hooray!

DIANA:
> Hooray!
> Gonna get back what I lost there.
> Gonna find out who I was.
> Gonna open up the gates and let it pour.

DAN:
> And if mem'ry makes things better,
> Well, mem'ry always does.
> Gonna get us back to better than before . . .

(They look through more keepsakes . . .)

DAN AND DIANA:
> Make ev'rything much better than before.

NATALIE:
> Won't anything be better than before?

DAN AND DIANA:
> Better than before.

DIANA:
> I guess it must be

DAN, DIANA AND NATALIE:
> Better than before
> Better than before . . .

(. . . when suddenly the music box ends up in Diana's hands. She looks at it a long moment before Dan realizes, and whisks it away. From the midst of the celebration, Gabe emerges. Lights. Music changes. Gabe speaks to Diana, and though she doesn't hear him, the others fade, leaving Diana alone.)

aftershocks

GABE:
> They've managed to get rid of me—return me to the
>   grave.
> ECT, electric chair—we shock who we can't save.

They've cleared you of my memory, and many more as
  well—
You may have wanted some of them, but who can ever
  tell?

Your brainwaves are more regular, the chemistry more
  pure;
The headaches and the nausea will pass and you'll endure;
Your son is gone forever, though, of that the doctor's sure.
The memories will wane . . .
The aftershocks remain.
You wonder which is worse—the symptom or the cure.

(Lights.
  Diana is at the kitchen table sorting through photos, papers,
more. Dan finds her.)

DAN: Diana? Honey? You've been at this for days.
DIANA: There's something missing, Dan. It's like it's tugging at
  me. I can almost see it.
DAN: Come to bed.

(He waits.)

If the memories are meant to come back . . . they will.

(A moment, and Dan goes.
  Diana gives a start, and hurries to the front door. She opens it to
Henry, almost knocking.)

HENRY: Oh. Sorry, Miz Goodman, I just needed to talk to Natalie
  about some homework.

(Diana just stares at him.)

I know it's late. She's not answering her . . . is everything all
  right?
DIANA *(Finding it)*: Henry.
HENRY: Yes?
DIANA: You remind me of someone. How old are you?

HENRY: Seventeen. Why?

DIANA *(Searches, then)*: I don't know. Natalie's in her room.

(Henry goes.
Diana watches him go.
Gabe watches her.)

GABE:

They've managed to get rid of me—I'm gone without a
trace,
But sear the soul and leave a scar no treatment can erase.
They cut away the cancer but forgot to fill the hole;
They moved me from your memory—I'm still there in
your soul.

Your life goes back to normal now, or so they all believe.
Your heart is in your chest again, not hanging from
your sleeve.
They've driven out the demons and they've earned you
this reprieve:
The memories are gone.
The aftershocks live on.
But with nothing to remember, is there nothing left to
grieve?

DIANA:

With nothing to remember . . .

(Lights. Music changes.
Natalie is in her room, not studying, when Henry slips in.)

hey #2

HENRY:

Hey.

NATALIE:

Hey.

HENRY:

So tomorrow's the dance.
It's annoying, I know,
But let's go.

NATALIE:

Not a chance.

HENRY:

Let me know you again.

—Okay, when?
Say wait, and I'll wait.

There's no way it's too late.

There's no way.

I stayed by your side . . .

Why do I get denied?

NATALIE:

Not right now—

It's already too late.

Hey—

Hey—will you listen?

Just shut up and listen.

You remind me of me . . .
And how fucked-up I can be.

HENRY:

Okay.
Hey.
Let's start over—clean slate.
I'll come by here at eight—
If you show,
Then we'll go.
If you don't, well, we'll see.

(He pulls the dance tickets from his pocket . . .)

NATALIE:

You just don't give up.

HENRY:

So don't give up on me.

(. . . and leaves one beside her.)

NATALIE:

Good-bye, Henry.

(A moment. Henry turns to go.
Lights.
Music changes.
Diana is with Doctor Madden.)

you don't know (reprise)

DIANA:

It's been four weeks since the treatment,
 and my mind is still a mess.
And what's left to be remembered,
 well, it's anybody's guess.
'Cause my past is like the weather—
 it will come and it will go.
I don't know
Even know
What it is that I don't know.

I'm some Christopher Columbus
 sailing out into my mind . . .
With no map of where I'm going,
 or of what I've left behind.

I don't know
The thngs I don't know.
I'm sure something's missing—
I wish it would show.
I don't know . . .
You say take it slow,
And I do, although
How I do
I don't know.

DOCTOR MADDEN:
 Are you talking with your husband?

DIANA:
 Well, he hasn't much to say.

DOCTOR MADDEN:
 Is it helping you remember?

DIANA:
 I remember that's his way.

DOCTOR MADDEN:
 Does the puzzle come together
 Piece by piece and row by row?

DIANA:
 I don't know
 I don't know
 Where the fucking pieces go.

 'Cause I don't know how this started,
 so I won't know when it's done.

DOCTOR MADDEN:
 Have you talked of your depression,
 your delusions, and your son?

(Music stops. This hangs there.)

DIANA: My what?

DOCTOR MADDEN: Your husband didn't— *(Stops himself, then)* I think
 you two . . . should talk more.

DIANA: We should talk more? That's it? I don't even remember
 marrying this man, it's not like I'm some sexually frustrated
 soccer mom.

DOCTOR MADDEN: Interestingly, the underlying challenges are
 similar. I'll see you next week.

DIANA: But—

DOCTOR MADDEN: Next week.

> *(Music. Doctor Madden goes.*
> *Diana steps out of the office, and is alone.*
> *Gabe appears, with the music box. He hands it to Diana, and*
> *she takes it without seeing him, and seems surprised to find it in her*
> *hands.*
> *She stands there.*
> *And then opens the box.*
> *Music changes.*
> *Gabe hums, wordlessly, with the music.*
> *Suddenly, Dan.)*

DAN: What are you doing?

> *(Diana shuts the music box.*
> *Music stops.*
> *Gabe disappears.)*

DIANA: What is this?
DAN: Where'd you get that? It's nothing, an old music box.

> *(He reaches for it, but Diana pulls it away. Music.)*

DIANA: We played it for the baby. Sometimes it helped him sleep.
DAN: Diana—
DIANA: Him. We did have a boy.
DAN: Diana. You—you shouldn't.

how could i ever forget?

DIANA:
> We were still living downtown . . .

DAN: It's not a good idea—

DIANA:

My black coat thrown over my blue nightgown . . .
You drove too fast—
The lights of the city flew past.

DAN: Please. Don't.

DIANA:

How could I ever forget?
Outside the morning was cool and wet.
He had such chills . . .
But still—he lay there so still.

And just eight months old . . .
So cold . . .

We ran him inside,
Lost—worrying, wondering.
That hospital room—
That gloom—

DIANA:	DAN:
How could I ever forget?	How could I ever forget?
Screaming at doctors—	God I was so upset.
alarmed, upset.	
They said to wait,	Diana—don't.
They never said we were	You think this will help,
too late.	but it won't.
But I was a child . . .	So many years ago . . .
Raising a child.	So much we could not
	know . . .

DIANA:

Those weeks full of joy . . .
Then—a moment of dread.
Someone simply said
Your child . . . is . . .

DIANA AND DAN:
How could I ever forget?
This was the moment my life was set.
That day that I lost you—
It's clear as the day we met.
How could I ever forget?

DAN: Why would you want to remember the things that hurt you?
DIANA: I want to remember everything, Dan. How did he die?
DAN: He was sick.
DIANA: With what? Why wasn't he treated? What was wrong?

DAN:
Something the doctors all missed,
The clinic, the ER, each specialist
They said, "Babies cry.
Allergies, gas, who knows why?"

And I was a child
Raising a child . . .

We stayed up all night . . .
Most nights you slept at his side.
But still he just cried
And cried . . .

DIANA *(Searching)*: He was a baby when he died. But I remember
him . . . older.
DAN: No. He was a baby. We should call Doctor Madden.

(Music changes.)

DIANA: Why would we call Doctor Madden? I'm just trying to make
sense of this. God—what was his name? I don't remember
ever hearing you say his name. Why is that?
DAN: Diana.
DIANA: What was his name? Tell me.

it's gonna be good (reprise)

DAN:

It's gonna be fine.
It's gonna be fine.
Gonna go back to the doctor,
'Cause we caught it just in time.
We'll take the pills and pay the bills

DIANA *(Over "pills")*: His name—

DAN:

We'll do more ECT.

DIANA *(After "ECT")*: Our son—

DAN:

It's gonna be good you'll see.

(A tuxedoed Henry appears at the open front door, and knocks. And knocks again. Finally, he makes his way inside.
After checking the time, Natalie starts downstairs from her room, with her dress peeking out from beneath a formal coat.)

DIANA:	DAN:
What was his name?	It's gonna be good, you'll see.
What was his name?	It's gonna be good
What was his name?	Gonna be good
What was his name?	Gonna be

(Natalie arrives downstairs. She glances briefly at Henry, before both of them turn their attention back to Diana and Dan.)

Name name name	Gonna be good good
Name name name	Good good

(Dan grabs the music box from her hands . . .)

DIANA:
What was his what was his name
What was his what was his name—

(. . . and dashes it to the ground. Silence.)

NATALIE: Jesus, Dad!

(She turns and runs back upstairs.)

DAN: Natalie!

(Henry is frozen a moment, then follows Natalie.)

why stay?

DIANA:
Why stay?
Why stay?
So steadfast and stolid
And stoic and solid
For day after every day . . .
Why stay?

Why stay?
Why not simply give in
And get on with livin',
'Cause everyone knows you tried—
But somehow something died
On the way.
So tell me why you stay?

(Split scene:
Henry gently opens Natalie's bedroom door.)

DIANA AND NATALIE:
Why stay?
Why stay?

Enduring and coping
And hurting and hoping
For day after fucking day—
Why stay?

Why stay?
Why not simply end it?
We'd all comprehend it,
And most of the world would say,
"He's better off that way,
To be free—
And maybe so is she."

a promise

DAN:

A promise,
A boy says forever . . .
A boy says,

DAN AND HENRY:

"Whatever may come, we'll come through.
And who can know how,
When all I know now
To be true
Is this promise that I make to you."

DAN:	HENRY:
A question,	
A boy wonders whether	A boy
The two stay together	Wonders
The way that they stay,	Should I stay?
For year after year,	Oh . . .
For love or from fear—	Oh . . .
Either way,	Either way . . .
That's the promise	
That I made that day	Here's what I say

DAN AND HENRY:

To the girl who was burning so brightly
Like the light from Orion above,

DAN:

And still I will search for her nightly—
If you see her, please send her my love.

DAN: HENRY:

And the boy was a boy
for all seasons—
The boy is long lost . . .
That boy is long lost to me now.
So lost . . .
And the man has
forgotten his reasons, Forgotten his reasons . . .

But the man still
remembers his vow. Now . . .

DAN:

A promise,
A man says forever.
A man says I'll never regret, or let you,
The promise I made
To stay, and I stayed true . . .
Knowing one day we'd remember that joy,
You'd remember that girl, I'd remember that boy,
Till we do
The promise I made
I'll make it brand-new—
The promise that I made to you.

(Dan and Diana are still.
Henry holds Natalie to him.
Two couples.
And then Gabe.
Music.)

i'm alive (reprise)

GABE:

> I am more than memory—
> I am what might be, I am mystery.
> Come closer . . .

DIANA: Dan.

(Gabe begins to approach Diana. Dan watches her back away.)

GABE:

> Come closer . . .

DAN: Diana, there's nothing there.

GABE:

> I'm old as time and forever young . . .
> I am every song that will stay unsung . . .
> I'll find you . . .

DIANA: Oh no.
DAN: God*damn* it!

GABE:

> Remind you . . .

(Diana turns toward the door.)

DIANA: Natalie!
DAN: Di—come back here!

(Diana bolts the room, and for a moment Gabe watches her go . . .)

GABE:

> Until you name me,
> You can't tame me—

(. . . and then he turns to Dan.)

This is one old game that I can play so well.

(Natalie leaves her room and meets Diana on the staircase, as Gabe pursues Dan.)

I'm alive
I'm alive
I am so alive—
And the medicine failed, and the doctors lied.
I'm alive
I'm alive
I am death defied—
I'm alive . . .
So alive . . .
I'm alive!

(Diana heads back down the stairs, slowly.
In Natalie's room, Henry waits patiently as she returns.)

NATALIE: I can't go to your dance. I have to take my mom to the doctor.
HENRY: I'll drive.
NATALIE: No.

GABE:
I'm alive.

HENRY: Let me help.
NATALIE: You can't.

(Downstairs, Diana grabs a coat and leaves.)

DAN: Diana!
NATALIE *(Hears this)*: Just go.

GABE:
I'm alive.

NATALIE: Look, I'll try to come later, okay?

HENRY: I'll wait for you there.
DAN: Natalie!

(Natalie goes, Henry follows.)

GABE:
　I'm alive.

(Lights. Music changes.
　Diana is with Doctor Madden. He's still in his coat, holding his keys.)

the break

DIANA:
　They told me that the wiring
　Was somehow all misfiring
　And screwing up the signals in my brain.

　And then they told me chemistry,
　The juice, and not the circuitry,
　Was mixing up and making me insane.

　What happens when the burn has healed
　But the skin has not regrown?
　What happens when the cast at last comes off
　And then you find the break was always in another bone?

DOCTOR MADDEN: Relapse is very common, Diana. It's upsetting that the delusional episodes have returned, but not entirely unexpected.

DIANA:
　They tried a million meds and
　They strapped me to their beds and
　They shrugged and told me, "That's the way it goes."

When finally you hit it,
I asked you just what did it—
You shrugged and said that no one really knows.

What happens if the medicine
Wasn't really in control?
What happens if the cut, the burn, the break
Was never in my brain or in my blood
But in my soul?

What happens if the cut, the burn, the break
Was never in my brain or in my blood
But in my soul?

make up your mind / catch me i'm falling (reprise)

DOCTOR MADDEN:
Make up your mind this is clarity—
Clarity that you did not have before.
The treatment is strong
But lasts only so long
It may be your mind's needing more.

DIANA: Let's say that's not it.
DOCTOR MADDEN: The ECT is powerful. It gave you your life back.
But the effects fade, and additional treatments are almost
always needed.
DIANA: That wasn't on the form.

DOCTOR MADDEN:
Make up your mind that you'll try again.
Make up your mind there are moments of light.
The one thing that's sure
Is that there is no cure—
But that doesn't mean we don't fight.

(Gabe enters, watching.)

DIANA:

    Catch me I'm falling . . .

DOCTOR MADDEN: We'll return to the talk therapy.

DIANA:

    Sinking and sprawling . . .

DOCTOR MADDEN: There's more work to do.

DIANA:

    Maybe I'll let myself fall.

DIANA AND GABE:

    Watch me I'm falling . . .

DOCTOR MADDEN: We might have to look at . . .

DIANA AND GABE:

    Maybe the falling . . .

DOCTOR MADDEN: . . . a new drug regimen.

(As Diana and Gabe continue:)

    There are other promising therapies. EMDR, for instance, or rTMS. Diana.

DIANA:	GABE:
Isn't so bad	Make up your mind
After all . . .	To be free.
Isn't so bad	Make up your mind
After all . . .	To be free.
Watch me I'm falling.	Make up your mind.
Watch me I'm flying.	Make up your mind.
Somehow surviving . . .	Make up—

DOCTOR MADDEN: Diana. You have a chronic illness. Like diabetes, or hypertension. If you leave it untreated, it could be catastrophic.

DIANA: I understand.

(Music changes.)

But there has to be another way.

DOCTOR MADDEN:
Stay with me.
Try again.
Don't walk out on treatment, don't lose what you've won—
You've struggled for years but you've only begun.

DIANA: My first psychiatrist told me that according to the manual, grief that continues past four months is pathological and should be medicated. Four months. For the life of my child. Who makes these decisions?
DOCTOR MADDEN: It's a guideline, nothing more.
DIANA: Yes. Nothing more.

DOCTOR MADDEN:
Stay with me.
Try again.
Is medicine magic? You know that it's not.
We know it's not perfect, but it's what we've got.
It's all that we've got.

DIANA: Good-bye, Doctor Madden.

*(She leaves the office and meets Natalie outside.
Music changes.)*

NATALIE: What'd he say?
DIANA: He said I could do more ECT or go back on the meds.
NATALIE: And what are you going to do?
DIANA: I'm going to take you to your dance.
NATALIE: Mom—
DIANA: It's time for you to start thinking of your own happiness.
NATALIE: It's not happiness. It's Henry.
DIANA: You love him.
NATALIE: Mom, you can't just walk out on your doctor.

maybe (next to normal)

DIANA:

Maybe I've lost it at last.
Maybe my last lucid moment has passed.
I'm dancing with death, I suppose . . .
But really—who knows?

Maybe I'm tired of the game,
Of coming up short, of the rules, of the shame—
And maybe you feel that way, too . . .
I see me in you.

A girl full of anger and hope,
A girl with a mother who just couldn't cope,
A girl who felt caught
And thought no one could see—
But maybe one day she'll be free

NATALIE:

It's so lovely that you're sharing.
No, really, I'm all ears.
But where has all this caring been
For sixteen years?
For all those years I prayed that
You'd go away for good—
Half the time afraid that
You really would.

When I thought you might be dying
I cried for all we'd never be.
But there'll be no more crying . . .
Not for me.

DIANA:

Things will get better, you'll see.

NATALIE:

Not for me . . .

DIANA:	NATALIE:
You'll see . . .	Not for me . . .
You'll see . . .	Not for me . . .
You'll see . . .	Not for me . . .

(Diana grabs Natalie, and holds her. A moment, then:)

DIANA:

Maybe we can't be okay.
But maybe we're tough, and we'll try anyway—
We'll live with what's real,
Let go of what's past,
And maybe I'll see you at last.

NATALIE: I don't believe you.

(Natalie turns to go. Diana watches her take a few steps, then:)

DIANA: Seventeen years ago your brother died of an intestinal obstruction. He was eight months old. I'm sorry we never talked about that. We wanted to give you a normal life, but I realize I have no clue what that is.

NATALIE:

I don't need a life that's normal—
That's way too far away.
But something . . . next to normal
Would be okay.

Yeah, something next to normal—
That's the thing I'd like to try.
Close enough to normal
To get by . . .

DIANA:

We'll get by.

NATALIE:

We'll get by.

DIANA: Okay. Now go to your dance.

(They go, separately.
Lights.
Music changes.
Henry is at the dance, alone, standing there.
Natalie arrives, coat off, showing her dress for the first time.)

hey #3 / perfect for you (reprise)

HENRY:

Hey.

NATALIE:

Hey.

HENRY:

You look like a star—
A vision in blue . . .

NATALIE:

Oh, I do?

HENRY:

And you are.
Hey—you came.

NATALIE:

Well I said that I might.

HENRY:

I thought we were through,
Me and you . . .

NATALIE:

Not tonight.

HENRY: NATALIE:
  Will your mom be okay?

                            Well, she might be, some day.
  But for now it's all fine?

                            She's still on my mind.
  Can you leave it behind?

                            Hey—
  Stay.

                            Hey—am I crazy?
  Let's see this thing through.

                            I might end up crazy.
  I'll be here for you.

NATALIE:
  You say that right here.
  But then give it a year,
  Or ten years, or a life—
  I could end up your wife.
  Sitting, staring at walls,
  Throwing shit down the stairs,
  Freaking out at the store,
  Running nude down the street,
  Bleeding out in the bath—

  (Henry grabs her and holds her.)

HENRY: Shh.

  *(He holds her a still moment. Then:
  Music changes.)*

  Perfect for you . . .
  I will be perfect for you.
  So you could go crazy,
  Or I could go crazy, it's true . . .
  Sometimes life is insane,
  But crazy I know I can do.

'Cause crazy is perfect,
And fucked-up is perfect,
So I will be perfect . . .

NATALIE:
Perfect . . .

NATALIE AND HENRY:
Perfect for you.

(They kiss.
Lights.
Music changes.
Dan sits, alone. Diana enters, with suitcases.)

so anyway

DIANA:
So anyway, I'm leaving.
I thought you'd like to know.
You're faithful, come what may,
But clearly I can't stay,
We'd both go mad that way—
So here I go.

And anyway, I'm leaving—
I guess that you can see.
I'll try this on my own.
A life I've never known.
I'll face the dread alone . . .
But I'll be free.

With you always beside me
To catch me when I fall,
I'd never get to know the feel of solid ground at all.

With you always believing
That we could still come through,
It makes me feel the fool to know that it's not true.

What doctors call dysfunction,
We tried to call romance.
And true, it's quite a trick to tell
The dancers from the dance—
But rather than let chance take me
I'll take a chance . . .

(Gabe enters, listening.)

I'll take a chance on leaving.
It's that, or stay and die.
I loved you once, and though
You love me still, I know
It's time for me to fly . . .

(She addresses both Dan and Gabe:)

I loved you once, and though
I love you still, I know
It's time for me to go . . .
And so good-bye.

*(She nods at Gabe, and goes.
Music changes.
Dan sits, unmoving, as Gabe approaches.)*

i am the one (reprise)

(To himself, after his wife:)

DAN:

I am the one who loved you.
I am the one who stayed.
I am the one, and you walked away.

I am the one who waited . . .
And now you act like you just don't give a damn—
Like you never knew who I am.

(Gabe moves slowly closer to Dan.)

GABE: DAN:
   I am the one who knows you.   I am . . .
   I am the one you fear.   I am . . .
   I am the one who's always   I've always been here.
      been here.

   I am the one who'll hear you.   I am . . .
   I know you told her that   I am . . .
   I'm not worth a damn,

GABE:
   But I know you know who I am.

DAN: No.

GABE:
   I know you know who I am.

DAN: Can't you just leave me alone?

GABE:
   I know you know who I am.

DAN: Why didn't you go with her?

GABE:
   'Cause I'm holding on . . .

DAN:
   Let me go.

GABE:
   And I won't let go . . .

DAN:
   Let me go.

GABE:
    Yeah, I want you to know

DAN:
    You don't know . . .

DAN AND GABE:
    I am the one who held you.
    I am the one who cried.
    I am the one who watched while you died.
    Yeah, yeah, yeah . . .
    I am the one who loved you.
    I tried pretending that I don't give a damn

GABE:
    But you've always known who I am.

DAN: Gabe. Gabriel.
GABE: Hi, Dad.

   *(Music ends.
      Natalie arrives home.
      Gabe disappears.)*

NATALIE: Dad? What the hell? Why are the lights off? Where's
   Mom?
DAN: She's, uh, she's . . .
NATALIE: Gone.
DAN: Yes.
NATALIE: Huh. So it's just me and you. For now.
DAN: Yes.
NATALIE: Okay.

   (Music.)

light

We need some light.
First of all, we need some light.
You can't sit here in the dark,
And all alone—
It's a sorry sight.
It's just you and me.
We'll live. You'll see.

(Natalie turns on a light.)

DAN:

Night after night
We'd sit and wait for the morning light.
But we've waited far too long
For all that's wrong
To be made right.

(Elsewhere, Diana appears.)

DIANA:

Day after day . . .
Wishing all our cares away . . .
Trying to fight the things we feel . . .
But some hurts never heal.
Some ghosts are never gone,
But we go on.
We still go on.

And you find some way to survive.
And you find out you don't have to be happy at all
To be happy you're alive.

*(Diana goes.
    Henry enters, on a different day. Calls off:)*

HENRY: Do you know where she went? Have you heard from her?

NATALIE: Oh, I've heard from her. She's staying with my grand-parents.

HENRY: Do they actually exist?

(Natalie has entered, not amused.)

NATALIE: Yes.

HENRY: So—that's good, right?

NATALIE: Well, going home has never been a solution to any of *my* problems.

HENRY: That's what you have me for.

NATALIE: Seriously? You're like number three on my list of issues.

HENRY: You keep a *list*?

NATALIE: But don't worry, Henry. You're my favorite problem.

HENRY: That's all I ask.

NATALIE:
Day after day,
Give me clouds, and rain, and gray.
Give me pain if that's what's real—

(Elsewhere, Doctor Madden is with Dan.)

NATALIE AND DOCTOR MADDEN:
It's the price we pay to feel.

DOCTOR MADDEN:
The price of love is loss,

(Natalie turns to go . . .)

But still we pay

(. . . but Henry pulls her back, and they kiss.)

We love anyway.

DAN: I know you can't tell me . . . if you're still treating her. I just, I wonder if she's okay.

DOCTOR MADDEN: I think she's working on it. And she's aware of the risks.

DAN: Do you think she'll come home?

DOCTOR MADDEN: It's hard to know.

DAN: Right.

DOCTOR MADDEN: Dan. Would you like me to recommend someone . . . for you to talk to?

DAN: Oh, no, I. Yes. I would. Thank you.

(They sit and talk, as Gabe appears elsewhere.)

GABE:

  And when the night has fin'ly gone,
  And when we see the new day dawn,
  We'll wonder how we wandered for so long, so blind.

(Dan and Doctor Madden stand. Doctor Madden writes on the back of a card, hands it to Dan . . .)

  The wasted world we thought we knew—
  The light will make it look brand-new.

(. . . and Dan leaves the office and steps out into the sunshine.)

NATALIE:	DIANA:	GABE AND DOCTOR MADDEN:	DAN AND HENRY:
Let it . . .	Let it . . .	So let it . . .	Let it . . .
So	So	Let it . . .	So
Let it . . .	Let it . . .	Let it . . .	Let it . . .
		Let it . . .	Let it . . .

(Elsewhere, Diana also steps into the sunshine.)

ALL:

  Shine!
  Shine!
  Shine!

Day after day . . .
We'll find the will to find our way,
Knowing that the darkest skies
Will some day see the sun—

DAN:

When our long night is done . . .

DAN AND NATALIE:

There will be light.

ALL :

There will be light . . .

When we open up our lives,
Sons and daughters, husbands, wives—
And fight that fight . . .
There will be light.

There will be light.
There will be light.
There will be light!

(Lights.)

THE END